CLASS DIFFERENCES
AND SEX ROLES
IN AMERICAN KINSHIP
AND FAMILY STRUCTURE

CLASS DIFFERENCES AND SEX ROLES IN AMERICAN KINSHIP AND FAMILY STRUCTURE

DAVID M. SCHNEIDER
RAYMOND T. SMITH
University of Chicago

PRENTICE-HALL, INC., Englewood Cliffs, New Jersey

Library of Congress Cataloging in Publication Data

SCHNEIDER, DAVID MURRAY
    Class differences and sex roles in American
kinship and family structure.

    Bibliography:
    1. Family—United States—Case studies. 2. Kinship
—United States—Case studies. 3. Social classes—
United States. I. Smith, Raymond Thomas,
joint author. II. Title.
HQ535.S332   301.42'1'0973   73–2582
ISBN 0–13–135046–3

© 1973 by Prentice-Hall, Inc.
Englewood Cliffs, New Jersey

Printed in the United States of America

10 9 8 7 6 5 4 3 2 1

Prentice-Hall International, Inc., *London*
Prentice-Hall of Australia, Pty. Ltd., *Sydney*
Prentice-Hall of Canada, Ltd., *Toronto*
Prentice-Hall of India Private Limited, *New Delhi*
Prentice-Hall of Japan, Inc., *Tokyo*

CONTENTS

PREFACE

In this book we report some of the findings of a study of kinship and family structure among lower-class people of Chicago,[1] and we have placed those findings in comparative association with our knowledge of middle-class kinship derived in part from Schneider's[2] and Smith's[3] earlier work as well as from our general knowledge of other sources.

A major aim of this book is to show how a particular theoretical treatment of culture, social system, and behavioral system might profitably proceed, for there has always been the problem of linking highly abstract conceptions of culture with the patterns of actual behavior.

The analysis of lower-class kinship is based upon data obtained from approximately 59 Afro-American, Southern White, and Spanish-American families living in Chicago (of which 40 provided relatively full information), but we have not hesitated

[1] The work was supported by a grant from the Childrens' Bureau numbered R328, and we gratefully acknowledge that support here.

[2] David M. Schneider, *American Kinship: A Cultural Account* (Englewood Cliffs, N.J.: Prentice-Hall, Inc., 1968); "Kinship, Nationality, and Religion in American Culture," in V. Turner, ed., *Forms of Symbolic Action, Proceedings of the 1969 Spring Meeting of the American Ethnological Society* (Seattle: University of Washington Press, 1969). Schneider's work was supported by grants from the National Science Foundation and by the National Institute of Mental Health, and this support is gratefully acknowledged here.

[3] Smith's comparative study of West Indian and American kinship was supported by the National Science Foundation.

to draw upon other sources when they were available.[4] In our interviews we sought two main types of data: the informant's spontaneous ideas about a wide range of topics in the kinship, occupational, and status domains, given in a series of interviews spread over a number of weeks or months, and a range of factual information on the informant's life history and on his kinsmen. Such interviews require that a long-term relationship with the informant be established, which in turn involves the interviewer in a measure of participant observation in the informant's community. Thus, although the number of our cases of Southern White and Spanish-American genealogies is small (11 and 9, respectively), they were obtained only after considerable involvement in neighborhood communities and in the context of more extensive field observation. Here we provide a general analysis based mainly on interviews and field observation, and we are now in the process of quantitative analysis of the genealogical information. We hope to present this material in a subsequent monograph.

Our treatment of many issues has been cursory. Starting from somewhat different viewpoints, we have tried to present the essentials of a theoretical position which is still in process of development. For example, our treatment of class is schematic in the extreme, and we have not been able to work through the details of case material in a manner that would demonstrate our every point in concrete and abundant detail. In the course of writing each of us has changed his viewpoint to greater or lesser degree and we fully expect to do so again. The problem of the status of the analytical distinction between culture, norms and behavior is a difficult one and we do not profess to have said the final word on the matter. We have tried to raise a series of issues in as clear a way as possible, and to point the direction toward their further discussion. For us the process has been rewarding in that we feel we now have a much clearer understanding of the basis of class differences in family and kinship relations, and we are totally convinced of the overwhelming importance of sex roles in those differences.

[4] Interviewing in Chicago was carried out over a period of several years and we are indebted to those, mostly students at the University of Chicago, who participated in this work.

CLASS DIFFERENCES AND SEX ROLES IN AMERICAN KINSHIP AND FAMILY STRUCTURE

INTRODUCTION

Chapter 1

One of the most durable topics in anthropology and sociology is the question of the universality of the nuclear family. It is theoretically satisfying and at the same time vaguely reassuring to suppose that all human beings share certain fundamental social and psychological characteristics. Still, there has been a growing suspicion that social scientists who find nuclear families everywhere may well be importing their own cultural preferences. European notions of what kinship really is do not necessarily accord with those of non-Europeans. The assumption that it is "natural" for women and immature children to be nurtured and protected by the woman's sexual mate is deeply embedded in European thought, and it is even believed that such an arrangement made it possible for culture to emerge as a distinctively human creation.

Scientific theories have progressed beyond the stage of supposing that any domestic arrangement which detaches children from their parents is "abnormal," but it is widely held that certain functional attributes of the nuclear family must be present for adequate socialization, e.g., small size, a differentiated sex-role structure, and generational or power differences.[1] Such attributes need not be located in "real" nuclear family members, provided

[1] Talcott Parsons and Robert F. Bales, *Family Socialization and Interaction Process* (Glencoe, Illinois: The Free Press, 1955), pp. 35–131.

that the functions are carried out by substitute role players.[2] The underlying conception is that something very like a nuclear family is the proper setting for domesticity and socialization.

Anthropologists are well aware of the discrepancy between the idea of the universality of nuclear families and the realities of life among such people as the Ashanti, the Nayar, or the Swazi. Special theories must be invoked, unless we are to consider whole societies to be deviant. Discussions of lower-class kinship in the United States generally assume that any variation from middle-class patterns is due to "disorganization," "deprivation," or "poverty." In the case of Afro-Americans it has been easy to regard slavery as the evil influence; for Whites who are "deviant," the attributed cause may be poverty, disruption caused by urbanization, by migration from the Old World, or imbalances in the ratio of males to females. Certainly it is generally supposed that all Americans value family life and would live like middle-class suburbanites if they could.

We wish to challenge that assumption, or at least question whether differences in family structure between classes are simply the product of poverty or disorganization. We contend that the lower class has a perfectly coherent and well-organized family system which differs from middle-class family structure; whereas middle-class norms attach positive value to the nuclear family as an independent entity, lower-class norms stress different patterns of solidarity, and lack the emphasis upon nuclear family isolation. Since we do not question the fact that all Americans share the same *kinship system*, including the concept of the family as a unit of husband, wife, and children, it becomes necessary to present at some length the analytical distinctions which encourage us to make such apparently contradictory statements.

We do not overlook the magnitude of the real problems of poverty, discrimination, and disorganization in American society,

[2] The germ of this idea is present in Malinowski's discussion of Australian and Trobriand family life, and it reappears in most "functionalist" interpretations of family structure,—e.g., Norman W. Bell and Ezra F. Vogel, Introduction to *A Modern Introduction to the Family* (Glencoe, Illinois: The Free Press, 1960).

particularly in the urban slums, but we do maintain that there is nothing *inherently* disorganized or abnormal about lower-class kinship and family life.[3] The reason it appears to be deviant is that, from the perspective of the social system as a whole, middle-class values encompass both lower- and upper-class values, and are proclaimed as the values of the entire system. While the upper class realize that their particular orientations are privileged and would not be good for everybody, the lower class both envy and defer to middle-class values without necessarily embracing them. Members of the lower class frequently explain their position in terms of the vicissitudes of their daily lives which prevent them from following middle-class patterns. Middle-class values are dominant, both in the sense that middle-class patterns are upheld by the forces of the society as a whole whenever they conflict with others, and in the sense that all classes pay symbolic deference to middle-class values while adhering to their own. This well-known discrepancy leads to the conclusion that lower-class behavior is somehow involuntary or perverse when contrasted with what people say they really *value*. If one turns the formula around, it can be seen that what people say they really value is a symbolic statement about the existential nature of the totality of social life.

Some Preliminary Theoretical Considerations

In this work we attempt to maintain a clear distinction between the cultural and social system levels of analysis of American kinship. The concept of "culture" has a complex history, and whereas many anthropologists see culture as an almost ad hoc collection of items, including patterns *of* behavior in a statistical sense, patterns *for* behavior in a normative sense, empirical generalizations

---

[3] It is important not to fall into the trap of reducing all class differences to a matter of "sub-culture," which is merely a descriptive device for saying that differences exist, and a means of avoiding the examination of the relations *between* classes. See Walter Miller, "The Elimination of the Lower Class as National Policy," in Daniel P. Moynihan (ed.), *On Understanding Poverty: Perspectives from the Social Sciences* (New York: Basic Books Inc., 1969), pp. 260–315.

about behavior, and so on, we propose to adopt the more restricted and precise definition advanced by Talcott Parsons. He suggests that culture be defined as a system of symbols and meanings, which, while they enter into and form an integral part of action processes, are nonetheless analytically separable from action and can be studied in isolation from it.[4]

In treating the cultural aspects of the kinship system it is fundamental to begin by asking, for each particular case, just what units it is built from, how those units are defined and differentiated in that culture, and how they are interrelated in that particular culture. It is essential for such a cultural analysis that the units be those which occur in that particular culture, and not those which are imposed on it by theories or assumptions about what kinship "really is" cross-culturally, or about its necessary or universal functions.

If a cultural analysis is to be of any value it must confine itself to the cultural material itself, for if the cultural level of analysis is irreducible and if culture is a major systemic component of social action, then it can be of no analytical utility if it is confused with other levels. Once the cultural material is clearly given and its structure determined, a systematic enquiry into its relation to social action, motivation, a functional analysis of change or maintenance of the system, and so on may be begun.

In the case of kinship and family structure, it is especially important to make clear the distinction between cultural and social structural levels of analysis, for many apparently "scientific" anthropological problems of kinship are produced through just such a confusion between a *particular* cultural definition of kinship, and certain apparently universal system processes dealing with physical and social reproduction. Since Lewis Henry Morgan, kinship has been regarded, by definition, as that system of social relations based on the relations of consanguinity and affinity. Hence kinship rela-

---

[4] See Talcott Parsons, *Societies* (Englewood Cliffs, N.J.: Prentice-Hall, Inc., 1966), Chap. Two, and T. Parsons, E. A. Shils, K. Naegele, and J. Pitts, eds., *Theories of Society* (New York: The Free Press, 1961), Vol. II, pp. 963–993.

tions could be viewed as genealogical relations, and the question asked of each culture is how this genealogical space is partitioned. Since all human beings reproduce sexually, and since the incest taboo is said to be universal, a kind of universal genealogical grid could be imagined as a model against which the particular system of any particular society could be compared. In one society kinship might only be counted up to and including third cousins. In another it might be extended patrilineally to a certain point, and matrilaterally only so far. Since kinship is, by definition of the analytical scheme, the system based on relations of blood and marriage, it is analyzed in just those terms; the many systems which happen not to conform to that definition are analyzed in those terms anyway.[5]

As we pointed out at the beginning of this chapter, a different theoretical tradition maintains that "the family" is a universal human institution, recognizable in every society as that group within which reproduction legitimately takes place, and within which the earliest care and socialization of children is carried out.[6] The American family is said to be a good example of this universal institution, since it is stripped of other functions which are extraneous to its essential nature. Whatever the strengths or weaknesses of this hypothesis, we must recognize that the units of description and analysis are defined by the analytical scheme, and therefore tend to guide observation in such a way as to by-pass the structure of the cultural system under study. Similarly, there are anthropological theories which assert that culture is a mechanism for adapting a particular people to a particular environment; a mechanism for solving certain basic and universal problems such as providing food, regulating sex, managing grief and suffering, or coordinating group activities. The tendency is to set up some sort of master chart listing "problems" along one axis and various "solutions" along the other.

---

[5] Meyer Fortes has drawn attention to this "genealogical fallacy" in his recent book, *Kinship and the Social Order: The Legacy of Lewis Henry Morgan* (Chicago: Aldine, 1969).

[6] George Peter Murdock, *Social Structure* (New York: The Macmillan Company, 1949); T. Parsons, *Family, Socialization and Interaction Process* (Glencoe, Illinois: The Free Press, 1955).

The difficulty with this procedure is not that it misrepresents the existence of problems, but that it fails to enumerate the problems defined by the culture itself, and thus arbitrarily assigns social action to the problem-solving sector given by the theory.

We assert that cultures not only adapt people to their environment, but also provide the conceptual framework through which the environment is experienced and social relations are mediated. They define the nature and components of the world, the units of which it is made up, and the meaning of those units. It is important, therefore, to ask *first* what problems are given by a particular culture, rather than assuming a priori that social action is oriented to the solution of general problems set by anthropological or sociological theory.

This does not mean that we advocate abandonment of general theory; on the contrary, it is general theory that urges us to stress the importance of the cultural system in understanding social action, and which leads us to treat it as an analytically separable element. That same general theory cautions us against treating *all* social action as a mere acting out of cultural norms, and purges the old-fashioned cultural theories of their reductionist tendencies. Nothing we have said should be taken to mean that we believe that the real world has no existence outside the categories of cultural systems. The problem of relating cultural analysis to other structural levels is inherent in our presentation, and we stress again our basic assumption that cultural elements are separable from action *only* for analytical purposes. They are "timeless categories" in that sense only.

The following chapter provides an outline of American kinship as a cultural system. This is a highly condensed and somewhat modified version of three of Schneider's earlier works,[7] which

[7] David M. Schneider, *American Kinship: A Cultural Account* (Englewood Cliffs, N.J.: Prentice-Hall, Inc., 1968); "Kinship Nationality and Religion," in V. Turner, ed., *Forms of Symbolic Action, Proceedings of the 1969 Spring Meeting of the American Ethnological Society* (Seattle: University of Washington Press, 1969); "What Is Kinship all About," in P. Reining, *Kinship Studies in the Morgan Centennial Year* (Washington, D.C.: Washington Anthropological Society, 1972), pp. 32–63.

the reader is urged to consult for a fuller understanding of the mode of analysis followed here. We then discuss the significance and meaning of class and ethnicity in American society from the point of view of its relevance to the contrasts we wish to draw between "middle" and "lower" class norms and behavior in those domains generally termed "family" and "kinship." We face a serious terminological problem here, since the term "kinship system" is most frequently used to refer to the system of interrelated norms governing action in kinship roles. It may even be used to refer to observed regularities of behavior, which is a different thing again.[8] In order to overcome this terminological difficulty we shall refer to the *pure* kinship system, the *normative* kinship system, and the *behavioral* system.

Just as one must distinguish these three ways of talking about kinship, so must one distinguish the nuclear family as a cultural symbolic system, as a normative system, and as a concrete group structure.

We argue that the differences between middle- and lower-class "kinship" and "family form" are not in fact differences in the "pure" kinship elements, including the structure of the "pure" familial system, but are differences at the normative level deriving from differences in the manner in which family structure articulates with other role systems, particularly with components derived from the occupational, class, and sex-role systems. In other words, it is our contention that what are normally thought of as family and kinship roles are actually compound or conglomerate roles which are analytically separable into "pure" kinship elements, sex-role elements, and elements derived from the system of status and class differentiation. This analytic procedure is more fully spelled out in the earlier Schneider works,[9] though the scheme presented here contains several modifications.

Before dissolving family and kinship roles into their constituent

---

[8] See M. Fortes, "Time and Social Structure: An Ashanti Case Study," in M. Fortes, ed., *Social Structure: Studies Presented to A. R. Radcliffe-Brown* (London: Oxford University Press, 1949), pp. 55–84.

[9] *American Kinship*, Chap. IV; "Kinship Nationality and Religion," pp. 117–123; "What Is Kinship all About," pp. 37–50.

components we present a model outline of the contrasted normative systems of the "middle" and "lower" class, in the relevant domains of kinship and family structure. We then try to demonstrate that such differences as exist between them derive primarily from variations in the nonkinship components.

In the final chapters we attempt to show how the cultural analysis of kinship and sex-role differentiation can throw light on some observed variations in behavior, and suggest a somewhat different way of approaching the study of problems in the area of familial and sexual behavior.

AN OUTLINE OF THE CULTURAL ASPECTS OF THE AMERICAN KINSHIP SYSTEM

Chapter 2

Perhaps the most important point to be made about the cultural aspects of American kinship is that there is a fundamental difference between *the distinctive features of kinship* and the *kinsman or relative as a person.* The former embodies those aspects which distinguish kinship from any other domain of American culture, such as commerce or politics, and which are necessarily present in any of its parts as these are further differentiated within the domain of kinship. Thus, although mother, father, brother, and sister are all different kinds of relatives, each is a kinsman (as opposed to the storekeeper, mayor, or policeman), and, as relatives, they all share the distinctive features of kinship.

Within the domain of kinship are two large, inclusive units. One is "family," the other is "relatives." Whereas "family" can mean all of one's relatives, "the family" is a unit which at the abstract level of cultural symbolism is formulated as husband, wife, and their child or children—all of whom are relatives, of course.

The nuclear family as a cultural symbolic system is deeply rooted in Judeo-Christian western culture. The idea of a man and a woman, united in carnal love for the production of children who are the embodiment of the physical substance of both parents, is a fundamental assumption about the nature of the reproductive process, and the conception of the family of parents and children is basic to religious doctrine and symbolism. In this sense it is concretized into vivid images, such as those of the Holy Family.[1] When we speak of the nuclear family as a cultural symbol we do not refer to these more dramatic presentations, which of necessity objectify the system by adding to it or modifying it; we refer to the elementary ideas which define what kinship is. At lower levels of normative structure and empirical groupings, "my family" or "immediate family" or even "the family" can mean something rather different with a different configuration of kinsmen.

The distinctive features of the domain of kinship in American culture can be abstracted from a consideration of the classification of the different kinds of relatives as well as from the family.

There are two kinds of relatives in American culture, those related "by blood" and those related "by marriage." A blood relationship is defined as the outcome of a single act of sexual intercourse which brings together sperm and egg and creates a child. Mother and father are thus related to the child by the fact that they create it and that the child is created out of the material substance which each contributes. "Blood" is thus a state of shared physical substance. This shared physical substance is, in this culture, an "objective fact of nature," a natural phenomenon, a concrete or substantive part of nature. And this objective fact of nature cannot be terminated. A blood relationship is a relationship of identity, and those who share a blood relationship share a common identity. The phrase "the same flesh and blood" is a statement of these beliefs.

While blood is a substance, a natural entity which endures in nature and cannot be terminated, "marriage" is exactly the opposite. It is not a material thing or substance in the same sense as biological heredity, nor is it a "natural thing" in the sense of a material object found free in nature. As a state of affairs it is, of course, natural, but it is not in itself a natural object, and it is terminable by death or divorce. Where blood is a natural material, marriage is not; where blood endures, marriage is terminable; and since there is no such

[1] See W. Lloyd Warner, *The Living and the Dead* (New Haven: Yale University Press, 1959), Chap. II.

"thing" as blood of which marriage consists, and since there is no such material which exists free in nature, persons related by marriage are not related "in nature."

If relatives "by marriage" are not related "in nature," how are they related? They are related by what Americans call "a relationship," that is, by the fact that they follow a particular code for conduct, a particular pattern for behavior. It is in this sense that a stepmother is not a "real" mother, not the genetrix, although she is in a mother–child relationship with her husband's child.[2]

The distinctive feature which defines the order of blood relatives is "blood," a natural substance, and blood relatives are thus "related by nature." This, it is suggested, is an instance within the larger class of *the natural order* of things as defined by American culture. That is, the natural order is the way things are in nature, and one class of things in the natural order consists in blood relatives.

Correspondingly, the feature which distinguishes relatives "by marriage" or "in law" is their relationship, the pattern for their behavior, the code for their conduct. This is an instance within the larger class of *the order of law,* which is opposed to *the order of nature.* The order of law is imposed by man and consists in rules and regulations, customs and traditions. It is law in its special sense, such as when a foster parent who fails to care properly for a child can be brought to court, and in its most general sense of law and order—custom, the rule of law, the government of action by morality and the restraint of human reason.

The domain of kinship, then, consists in two major parts, each of which is but a special case of the two major orders of which the world is composed, the order of nature and the order of law. It is this division which makes sense of the fact that those who are relatives by marriage are also called in-laws, for they are related in the order of law, not in the order of nature.

---

[2] In the West Indies such a woman is sometimes referred to as a mother-in-law, which is a logical term. Whether such usage is common in parts of the United States we do not know.

The complete typology of kinds of relatives distinguished by American culture is built out of these two elements: *relationship as natural substance* and *relationship as code for conduct.*

Turning now to *the family,* the picture of the distinctive features of kinship in American culture can be completed. Family and relatives are coordinate categories in American kinship in that they share one of their meanings, though certain of their other meanings diverge. Every member of the family is at the same time a relative, and every relative is, in this sense, a member of the family. But the word "family" is singular, not plural. In its singular form, and at the most general conceptual level, it includes at least three different kinds of family members. The word "relative" in the singular can mean only one person or one kind of relative. The term "family" thus serves to assemble certain different kinds of relatives into a single cultural unit; this meaning is quite different from the simple plurality of relatives, without regard to their kind or to their relationship, to each other, and it is different from "family" used to mean an aggregate of kin who live together. Not only are there different kinds of relatives assembled into a single cultural unit, but they are in a very special relationship, for they are husband, wife, and child, or father, mother, and child to each other. Since members of the family are kinds of relatives, the distinctive features in terms of which relatives are defined and differentiated are the same as those which define and differentiate the members of the family on the one hand, and the family as a cultural unit on the other.

Sexual intercourse is the symbol which provides the distinctive features in terms of which both the members of the family as relatives and the family as a cultural unit are defined and differentiated.

Blood is a matter of birth, birth a matter of procreation, and procreation a matter of sexual intercourse. Sexual intercourse as an act of procreation creates the blood relationship of parent and child and makes genitor and genetrix out of husband and wife. Sexual intercourse is an act in which, and through which, love is expressed; it is often called "making love," and love is an explicit cultural symbol in American kinship.

There are two kinds of love in American kinship. One can be

called *conjugal love*, the other *cognatic love*. Conjugal love is erotic, having the sexual act as its concrete embodiment. Cognatic love on the contrary is not an act but a state of affairs and marks the blood relationship, the identity of natural substance which obtains between parent and child. Cognatic love has nothing erotic about it. The conjugal love of husband and wife is the opposite of the cognatic love of parent, child, and sibling. One is the union of opposites, the other the unity of identities, the sharing of biogenetic substance.

The symbol of "love" links conjugal and cognatic love together and relates them both through the symbol of sexual intercourse. Love in the sense of sexual intercourse is a natural act with natural consequences, according to its cultural definition, and at the same time stands for unity. This unity arising from sexual intercourse based on love is prior to the concept of the legality of marriage, so that a couple can think of themselves as being "truly married" even though they are not legally married.

The facts of biological relatedness and sexual relations play a fundamental role in American kinship, for they are the material out of which American culture formulates the symbols in terms of which a system of social relationships is defined and differentiated. Beliefs about the facts of biological relatedness and sexual relations constitute a model from which a series of postulates about the nature of that domain of social relationships called kinship are derived and stated. The statement of identity in terms of flesh and blood between mother and child, whatever significance the actual biological relations may have, is at the same time a symbolic statement of the kind of social relationship which should obtain between them.

The different symbols of American kinship are all concerned with unity of some kind: the unity of those related by blood, those joined in love, the parent and child in the face of the child's growing up and going off to found a family of his own, man and woman as husband and wife, and so on. All of these different kinds of unity are expressed as the unity of substance or the unity required by a code for conduct.

Put somewhat differently, all of the symbols of American kinship seem to say one thing: they provide for relationships of diffuse, enduring solidarity ("diffuse" because they are functionally diffuse rather than specific, in Parson's sense of the term).[3]

In contrast to a "job," which is intended to get some specific thing "done," there is no specific limitation on the aim or goal of any kinship relationship. Instead, the goal of the relationship is "solidarity," the "good" or "well-being" or "benefit" of ego with alter. Whatever is "good for" the family, the spouse, the child, the relative, is the "right" thing to do. The relationships are enduring in the generalized sense symbolized by "blood"; there is no built-in termination date. Indeed, such a relationship simply is, and *cannot* be terminated. Although a marital relationship can be terminated by death or divorce, it is supposed to endure and persevere and not be regarded as transient, temporary, or conditional. This is clearly stated in the wedding oath "till death do us part," and professions of eternal love characteristically mark relations between lovers, unless those relations are considered shallow and unworthy.

The phrase "diffuse, enduring solidarity" is not used by American informants, of course, and although many of them understand it when it is explained to them, it sounds to them, as it should, like jargon. Meyer Fortes has discussed kinship in terms which are not very different from those presented here. He has his own jargon, however, preferring to refer to "kinship amity" or "prescriptive altruism," rather than "diffuse, enduring solidarity." He says "Kinship predicates the axiom of amity, the prescriptive altruism exhibited in the ethic of generosity." [4]

This, in brief summary, is the domain of kinship as defined by its distinctive features, those aspects which distinguish kinship from all other domains of American culture. This domain can be treated in a number of different ways. It can be considered in those analytic terms described by the jargon, "diffuse, enduring solidarity."

[3] Talcott Parsons, *The Social System* (New York: The Free Press, 1951), p. 66.

[4] Meyer Fortes, *Kinship and the Social Order: The Legacy of Lewis Henry Morgan* (Chicago: Aldine, 1969), p. 237. See also his book *The Web of Kinship among the Tallensi* (London: Oxford University Press, 1949).

It is that cultural system of diffuse, enduring solidarity which is defined and differentiated from other domains in terms of the symbol of coitus, where the biogenetic identity of the parent and child stand for a relationship of diffuse, enduring solidarity—which is called "love" in American culture. The embrace of the husband and wife, the act of love, making love, stand for what is called here, in jargonese, "conjugal love." The domain is defined by a single symbol, coitus, which can be expressed in a variety of different ways, and a variety of different forms, but which has two aspects, each of which stands for *unity*.

The family in the sense outlined here is a paradigm for what each relative is, and how they should behave toward each other. Its members are united by blood or by licit sexual relationship, and their relationship to each other is one of love, either conjugal or cognatic, but in either it is a relationship of diffuse, enduring solidarity. The actual structuring of the whole range of categories of kinsmen and their mode of relationship to each other does not concern us directly in this monograph, though we shall have occasion to refer to some aspects of the patterning of wider solidarities in Chapter 5.

Though it is possible to conceive of kinship in these abstract terms, and informants are sometimes able to discuss it in this way, it is more usual to deal at a lower level of specification with relatives thought of as "persons" acting within what is thought of by anthropologists as the kinship domain. As we mentioned in Chapter 1, we are confronting a difficult terminological issue; if we restrict kinship to its pure form, defined and differentiated in terms of its distinctive features, we are apt to confuse it with that from which we wish it to be distinguished—namely, the lower level normative prescriptions which define and differentiate proper action for persons who are kin to each other, but whose actions are simultaneously governed by nonkinship considerations. Long before we concern ourselves with individuals and their behavior, we must consider "persons," that is, cultural constructs which identify the major characteristics of role players in systems of social action. "The family" can, in one of its meanings, refer to an action system involving a group of persons. Such persons are cultural constructs whose configuration is derived from a blending of elements from diverse domains of the cultural system.[5]

A further complication arises. Formal sociology has developed a complex series of categories, such as "role," "status," and "institution," which, it is believed, can be used to classify forms of human social behavior. We wish to suggest, however, that whatever the observed uniformities of behavior, whatever order can be teased out of statistics, social structure exists at a different level. An actor, or a series of interacting persons, have available a complex system of cultural elements from which they can construct a model of appropriate proper behavior for any context or situation. The first task of anthropology, as we see it, is to analyze the structure of the cultural categories utilized in the construction of such models, and to show how the actions of individuals are conditioned both by the structure of these cultural systems, by the contingencies of social system integration or conflict, and the manner in which those actions lead to a reformulation of cultural models. That is, we must analyze culture in action, recognizing a clear difference between the relative stability of shared meanings and understandings, and the variable projection of them in concrete action situations.

To this end we suggest that a two-stage approach be adopted. First, it is desirable to analyze the nature of the cultural constructs themselves. This was attempted by Schneider with special reference to urban middle-class kinship.[6] He suggested that the person may be thought of as the cultural definition of the actor in a social system. The "person" would be distinguished from such well-known sociological categories as "role" and "status" by virtue of the fact that it is analyzed solely from the cultural point of view, leaving open its relationship to "role," which is specifically treated as a link among cultural, social, and personality levels of analysis. This dis-

---

[5] The configuration of the cultural construct of the person may be ultimately determined by, or affected by, the functional requirements of the social system. This is clearly a point at which cultural configuration and social system requirements intersect, and there is likely to be disputation as to which is "prior" or "determinative." This is not an issue we care to go into here.

[6] David M. Schneider, *American Kinship: A Cultural Account* (Englewood Cliffs, N.J.: Prentice-Hall, Inc., 1968).

tinction ensures that levels of system analysis are kept unequivocally clear, but it is by no means easy to accomplish.

The "person" is thus constructed out of symbols and definitions from various cultural domains, but he is constructed in relation to particular contexts and systems. For example, the father as a person capable of acting (or rather capable of being a cultural model for action) is distinguished from the pure kinship definition of father as genitor by the fact that he is specified in more concrete terms. He is a person of defined age, occupation, sex-role attributes, and so on. At this level there are marked variations in the structure of the persons who constitute families, and in the structure of the family as a group in America. Such variations appear to be closely associated with class differences, and they exist even if household composition of the various classes is the same.

At the risk of appearing repetitious, we may set out the hierarchy of analysis yet again. First we abstract the distinctive features of kinship and treat these as the defining characteristics of the "pure" system which sets off kinship from all other cultural domains. We then argue that, at a lower level of specification, kinsmen are culturally constructed as persons with combinations of different attributes which define the manner in which action can take place. The person in this sense is the culturally defined aspect of social role, but we argue that there is some merit in trying to keep this aspect distinct, at least in the beginning. The person is a unit capable of action, and although his primary identity may be located in the kinship field, he is made up of elements from such other domains as sex-role, age differentiation, class, and occupation. Different elements are blended together to make up the definition of the person, but such elements must make up a unit defined as potentially doing something, playing a role in real life. The elements come from different systems of concepts and symbols, each from its own domain, which is defined apart from persons or other such qualifications. For instance, informants say that a wife cooks and keeps house; does the wife do this because she is a *wife* or because she is a *woman?* Once the question is asked, the informants are quite clear that she cooks and keeps house because she is a woman.

Women who are not wives cook and keep house, and wives do not necessarily cook and keep house. These acts do not make a woman a wife. The distinctive feature which defines a wife is that she is the legitimate sexual partner of her husband.

Kinship and family at this more specific, model-for-action level, is therefore a complex of interacting roles, many dimensions of which are nonkinship in the more abstract "pure" sense.

CLASS AND ETHNICITY: THE BACKGROUND TO KINSHIP VARIATION

Chapter 3

It is sometimes said that the United States is a classless society, but this is always a statement of intent, designed to separate American society as a type from the class-ridden Old World societies from which most Americans are descended. Some antipathy to class consciousness remains, but few Americans deny the existence of social classes in their society; most like to think of themselves as being "middle class," which is perhaps indicative of the wish to escape into classlessness by a peculiarly neutral route.[1] In this monograph we do not profess to explore the complexities of the American class system, either at the cultural or social system levels. We beg many difficult questions by simply regarding the middle class as a broad but not undifferentiated category which includes those who have certain attitudes, aspirations, and expectations toward status mobility, and who shape their actions accordingly. The lower and the upper classes are at rest, relatively speaking. They do not act as though they seriously believe that they are headed "up" or "down,"

---

[1] R. W. Hodge and D. J. Treiman, "Class Identification in the United States," *American Journal of Sociology*, 73, No. 5 (1968). This national sample survey shows that, in unstructured questioning, fully three-quarters of the sample identified with some variety of "middle class." In a precoded question 2.2 per cent identified with the upper class, 2.3 per cent with the lower class, 16.6 per cent with upper middle, 44.0 per cent with middle, and 34.3 per cent with the "working class." The last was rarely resorted to when respondents were asked to provide their own categories for self-identification.

although certain individuals may harbor fantasies of sudden wealth or poverty, and even act in terms of those fantasies. It is true that all lower-class people in this society, as in most others, yearn for an improvement in their physical condition. This is very different from the calculating attempts of the middle class to move up the ladder of success by the solid virtues of thrift, hard work, and calculated self-interest. As one of our informants said, "To be a square dude is hard work, man."

Class as a Cultural Construct

The tendency to think of society as divided into three classes is at least as old as Aristotle, but the modern urban and suburban middle class is a relatively new phenomenon. Karl Marx and Max Weber laid the groundwork for the analysis of the emergence and historical role of the modern middle class, and although it might be difficult to recognize the hero-villains of the rise of the bourgeoisie, the growth of capitalism, and the emergence of the Protestant Ethic in the average suburban commuter, he is nonetheless the embodiment of a particular cultural tradition, developed in particular historical circumstances.

That cultural tradition can be brought into sharp focus by considering the question of individualism, which is often thought of as a particularly American characteristic. A gross comparison between the ideology of Indian caste society and that of the Euro-American Judeo-Christian tradition points up the emphasis upon the individual (or the "person") as the unit of action in the latter, as opposed to the corporate status group in traditional India. This contrast has been drawn sharply by Dumont,[2] but the main argument is not new. The transformation of European societies from collections of closed estates to relatively open class societies was

[2] See L. Dumont, *Homo Hierarchicus* (Chicago: The University of Chicago Press, 1970); "Caste, Racism and 'Stratification,' " *Contributions to Indian Sociology*, No. V (October 1961), pp. 20–43.

accompanied by the growth of complex ideologies which ranged from religious doctrines, such as Calvinism, to classical economic theory and modern political nationalism, all of which emphasize the rational individual as the fundamental moral entity out of which society is composed through individual acts of association. Dumont argues brilliantly that even doctrines of the corporate state, such as those of German National Socialism, are ultimately predicated upon a view of society as a collection of individuals, rather than as a true organic entity.

American culture is not merely heir to this tradition, but is perhaps its most extreme expression. A constant stream of European writers, of whom de Tocqueville is merely the best known, have looked to the United States for an image of Europe's future—if not the future of the world—and all have been impressed by the sentiments of egalitarianism and individualism, and their expression in forms of social life apparently so different from those of Europe.

What is variously termed "the American Creed," the "dominant value system," or the "ideal system" clearly embodies this ideological stress upon the contradictory values of equality and individual status achievement or mobility. Lloyd Warner, for example, says:

> In the bright glow and warm presence of the American Dream all men are born free and equal. Everyone in the American Dream has the right, and often the duty, to try to succeed and to do his best to reach the top. Its two fundamental themes and propositions, that all of us are equal and that each of us has the right to the chance of reaching the top, are mutually contradictory, for if all men are equal there can be no top level to aim for, no bottom one to get away from. . . .[3]

Seymour Martin Lipset has documented at length the proposition that the United States is dominated by the values of egalitarianism

---

[3] W. Lloyd Warner, Marcia Meeker, and Kenneth Eells, *Social Class in America* (New York: Harper Torchbooks, 1960), p. 3.

and achievement, and that these values have, through the interplay of their contradictions, been instrumental in shaping American institutions. He says:

> The value we have attributed to achievement is a corollary to our belief in equality. For people to be equal they need a chance to become equal. Success, therefore, should be attainable by all, no matter what the accidents of birth, class, or race. Achievement is a function of equality of opportunity. That this emphasis on achievement must lead to new inequalities of status and to the use of corrupt means to secure and maintain high position is the ever recreated and renewed American dilemma.[4]

The most extreme conclusion which has been drawn from these observations is that America is essentially a classless society characterized by a continuous rank-order scale upon which individuals are ranged according to objective criteria stressing individual performance. Individuals may then be grouped into a number of categories, sometimes called "classes." This is a use of the term very different from that which stresses the group nature of social class, whereby classes are, or may become, self-conscious, acting units.

The most difficult problem encountered in this view of American society as essentially classless, open, mobile, and achievement-oriented is the position of the so-called "nonwhite" population of Blacks, American Indians, Mexican-Americans, Puerto Ricans, and Asiatics. Lipset asserts that "American egalitarianism is, of course, for white men only. The treatment of the Negro makes a mockery of this value now as it has in the past." [5] Dumont manages to make the best of the difficulty by arguing that racism is a disease of democracy; it is *only* where individualism is the encompassing value that individuals are systematically discriminated against on the basis of physical characteristics.[6] Such simple ignoring of the socioeco-

[4] Seymour Martin Lipset, *First New Nation* (New York: Anchor Books, Doubleday & Co., Inc., 1967), p. 2.

[5] Lipset, *First New Nation*, pp. 379–380.

[6] Dumont, "Caste, Racism and Stratification," 38–43.

nomic context in which racial discrimination has developed in the United States is only possible when one is exclusively concerned with the logical structure of values and ideologies, but it is precisely those politicoeconomic contexts which we must examine if we are to understand the way in which class and ethnicity affect the construction of kinship roles.

To see Blacks, or other ethnic groups, as being outside the "mainstream" is another, and related, way of resolving the problem. The poor can also be placed in this marginal, residual, or peripheral position in which they become a social aberration, marked by a "culture of poverty," "disorganization," "a tangle of pathology," or some other negative, abnormal bundle of characteristics. Such a view depends upon the analyst's taking his position in the mainstream, or at the center, and by-passes any objective analysis of the content of the cultural system of the supposedly peripheral groups. In fact, it is not an exaggeration to say that these theories are really an integral part of middle-class ideology.

Not all analysts view the United States as a classless society. Lloyd Warner's well-known study of Newburyport, Massachusetts, took quite the opposite view, and argued that it is not only possible to sort the population of American towns and cities into classes, but that these are recognized to exist by the inhabitants themselves, so that class is rooted in the consciousness of Americans as well as in the objective facts of their existence.[7] Richard Centers' study was one of the best-known attempts to demonstrate the reality of class consciousness in American society,[8] and Kornhauser's follow-up survey, while it did not entirely confirm Centers' assertions, certainly demonstrated the existence of significant variations in attitude and belief among income and occupational groups.[9]

---

[7] W. Lloyd Warner and Paul Lunt, *The Social Life of a Modern Community* (New Haven: Yale University Press, 1945).

[8] Richard Centers, *The Psychology of Social Classes* (Princeton: Princeton University Press, 1949).

[9] Arthur Kornhauser, "Public Opinion and Social Class," *American Journal of Sociology*, 55 (1950), pp. 333–345. See also John C. Leggett, *Class, Race and Labor* (New York: Oxford University Press, 1968).

sues at stake here are considerable, for they involve the
ions of the nature of the society, internal variations in
culture, and the manner in which cultural symbols are
articulated with action in the most strategic areas of the social
system.

It could be argued that the American class system is precisely
that system of continuous rank gradation which is seen by the broad
middle as the normal outcome of the operation of individual
achievement. The system would thus be an expression of the logical
principles which inhere in the cultural definition of equality and
achievement. The significant unit in the system is the individual,
unfettered by family or other group affiliation, afforded equality of
opportunity to make himself into the "best" expression he can
of the most valued characteristics of the society. What are those
most valued characteristics? Here we come face-to-face with a most
interesting fact. Just as an individual's position on the scale of rank
is not determined by ascribed characteristics, that is, by his intrinsic
qualities, so there are no fixed standards of behavior which serve to
mark status. The only clearly defined cultural standards against
which status can be measured are the gross standards of income,
consumption, and conformity to rational procedures for attaining
ends. There is a constant search for new ends which are defined as
desirable because they are in conformity with a rationally elaborated
image of the meaning of the world, which image is constantly liable
to change because of the discovery of new "facts."

The cultural values of equality and achievement, important
though they are as components of the American status system, are
derived from the more general cultural stress upon individualism.
The importance of "the person" as a cultural construct was touched
upon in Chapter 2. In American culture, the person is defined as
the basic unit of action, rather than the group, the aggregate, or
the collectivity. When some larger assemblage is involved, it is
personified, and thus redefined as a person capable of acting or
doing things. In law a corporation can be treated as a person and
held responsible for its acts quite apart from the acts of any of its

officers. But even when corporate groups or collectivities are personified in this way, the relationship between the unit and any member is such that the member's whole social identity is never defined by his membership in that unit alone. The emphasis in American culture is upon dealing with the person on his own merits as a unique individual, despite whatever associations he may have. The ideal is that each person's identity, his position, should derive from his own actions and not from the actions of any group with which he may be associated.

American society, like any other, is faced with organizational problems which require a subjugation of individual desire to collective ends. Although the cultural stress is upon the person as the significant unit of action, this does not mean that social structure is merely the outcome of a series of individual acts unconstrained by normative factors and situational exigencies. It is precisely the tension between cultural stress upon the individual as the unit of action, and the necessity for a very complex organizational structure which makes class such a difficult concept to deal with in this case.

"Social class" in American culture is not conceived as a closed corporate entity whose members have a special rank within the society by virtue of their membership in that group, a rank which can change only when the formal rank of the whole group changes within the system. Such a closed entity is represented by a caste in Hindu culture. In America, a person's membership in a particular class is thought to depend upon his actions and their conformity to class standards.

We said earlier that the standards of class are difficult to describe because they are not fixed. Apart from size of income and scale of consumption, there are no clear markers of class, a fact which is closely related to the absence of fixed groups.

However, there is a differential cultural stress upon the selection of ends and the mode of evaluating means for attainment of ends. The culturally middle-class value for judging both ends and the relationship between means and ends is the value of *rationality*. In this context, application of the value of rationality involves the use of universalistic standards in making choices.[10] The culturally lower-class value lays stress upon *security*, a procedure which involves the use of particularistic standards and traditional criteria. Upper-class values do not stress security, but they do emphasize particularistic standards, stability, and continuity or "tradition" in a way that has more in common with lower- than with middle-class culture.

Culturally, then, "class" takes its structure from the primacy of evaluation placed upon different modes of relating ends to means.

These cultural characteristics do not exist apart from their bearers, no matter how analytically expedient it may be to represent them in this way, and the bearers of cultural values are concrete individuals involved in a multiplicity of social relationships. As such, they activate different, and perhaps contradictory, values at different times. For all Americans rationality is an active element in the norms of action, but we recognize a lower-class cultural complex by the fact that rationality is subordinated to the dominant value of security, and its traditionalistic, particularistic concomitants. We thus expect to find, in the lower class as in the upper class, rationality harnessed to the service of traditionalistic, particularistic ends and means. In the middle class the opposite obtains, with traditionalistic, particularistic elements being harnessed in the service of rationality, permitting its free application to limited areas while other areas are maintained in a given position. But in each case one set of values is held primary, with the other in a secondary position; the one encompasses the other, and it is this relationship that yields the striking differences in cultural orientation among classes.

The cultural system of class thus depends upon the secular nature of the social order, on the predominance of the person rather than the group as the unit which is conceptualized and evaluated in the system, on the value of equality predominating over (though not eliminating) the value of hierarchy, and upon the premise that

[10] Needless to say, this view of "class" derives from the dominating ideology of American society, that of bourgeois individualism. It does not speak to the historically important issue of class conflict, which requires a different mode of analysis.

the person is, or should be, autonomous. That is he should be free to pursue his ends in a rational manner, unencumbered by family, fate or station in life.

It is worth repeating that classes, even at the cultural level, are not isolates. They constitute part of a wider order or system of classes which are always thought of in relation to each other. In this wider context class values are ranked, or, more properly, are accorded significance in proportion to their appropriateness for the continuation of the society as a whole in its present form. From this perspective middle-class values can be said to encompass both lower- and upper-class values. This is particularly clear as regards the lower class, where considerable deference is paid to middle-class values, and where people often explain their inferior position in terms of circumstances which have prevented them from behaving in a middle-class fashion. That is, in contrast to middle-class norms of rationality, lower-class norms of security and tradition are judged inferior even by members of the lower class. Upper-class values of tradition and particularism are also considered to be "wrong," or at least an indulgence, when contrasted with middle-class values of rationality. The upper class sees itself as a privileged stratum which really ought to pay deference to middle-class values because they are the driving force of the whole social system. While the upper class may take advantage of particularistic ties in order to achieve individual ends, its members do not attempt to alter institutions to accord with upper-class values; on the contrary, they are the staunchest upholders of the norms of rationality and achievement—for others.

Class as a Dimension
of the Social System

Shifting from the cultural to the social structural level, one can see that American society is made up of a series of interrelated organizational structures, highly differentiated and specialized. Virtually all studies of status ranking in the United States emphasize occupation as the primary determinant of social position. Since there is no single univalent rank order, we would not expect to find a perfect scale of occupational prestige. But we do discover that, in this highly urbanized, industrialized society, the occupational milieu is the important formative influence so far as class culture is concerned.

As we pointed out, concern with the structure of American values, "national identity," or "American character" leads many writers to view the United States as an essentially classless society. The fact that most Americans will choose, under certain circumstances, to identify with the middle class is taken as evidence of the fact that recognition of rank or gradation of status does not lead to the formation of disjunctive classes. There is acknowledgment of a lower class, but, as Gunnar Myrdal observed, this could more properly be designated an "under-class that is not really an integrated part of the nation but a useless and miserable substratum." [11] Theories of the "culture of poverty" take a similar view of this "external" and self-perpetuating group which has a particular culture shaped by the degeneration of its social condition.

Rather than class consciousness in contemporary American society, one finds a multiplicity of overlapping status groups based upon occupation, income, style of life, ethnicity, and race. Still, we have been able to distinguish markedly different clusters of attitudes which find expression in kinship and family behavior, and the contrasts in these attitudes are most sharp between well-off professional, managerial, and white-collar workers and poor, unemployed, partially-employed, or unskilled workers. We have thus far referred to the lower, middle, and upper classes, but this is a preliminary orienting use of these terms which merely points the way toward a more detailed examination of the empirical variations in status and in associated cultural patterns.

At the very center of our assumptions is a recognition of differences between social classes which are more than differences of

[11] Gunnar Myrdal, *Challenge to Affluence* (New York: Pantheon Books, Inc., 1963).

position upon some objective scale of ranking. There are differences of life style and of culture, though we do not share the common anthropological tendency to confuse "subculture" with the existence of differentiated groups. On the contrary, it seems to us that it is possible neither to construct univalent scales of rank or prestige which serve to divide American society into disjunctive strata,[12] nor to divide American society into a series of clearly bounded and relatively self-contained groups which are the bearers of distinctive subcultures. The cultural differences to which we refer are parts of a single system which varies according to internally consistent logical principles, and are, at the same time, an expression of the different and varying life experiences of individuals, particularly in relation to the occupational milieu. These cultural differences are not isolated from each other; they are available to all individuals. In general they are present in all individuals as potential means of constructing social reality, though the emphasis and mode of patterning varies in a systematic way between classes.

One must avoid the error of assuming that the cultural system is unchanging. It is precisely the varying experiences of social groups which lead to the institutionalization of new symbolic orientations. In order to anchor our discussion at a more concrete level, we now turn to a brief examination of the social background of the families we studied.

Class and Ethnicity in Chicago

The field investigations on which this study is based were carried out in Chicago, a city unlike any other in many respects, but in some ways not unrepresentative of the growing urban areas of the United States. More than two-thirds of all Americans now live in towns and cities, many of them much smaller than Chicago, but

[12] See Edward A. Shils, "Deference," in John A. Jackson, ed., *Social Stratification* (Cambridge: Cambridge University Press, 1968), pp. 104–132, for an excellent discussion of the multiple and overlapping bases of prestige evaluations and the impossibility of constructing simple univalent rankings.

still sharing some of its general characteristics.[13] Many of these city dwellers are immigrants, for it is characteristic of American cities that their populations are in constant motion, and of nowhere is this more true than of Chicago.[14]

In 1910 more than half of the population of Chicago had been born outside the United States.[15] Migration into the midwest increased rapidly after the opening of a direct rail connection from New York in 1853, and the first flow of new immigrants were mainly Irish, German, Norwegian, and Swedish, as well as some longer-settled Americans of English and Scots ancestry. After 1875 the immigrant flow from Southern and Eastern Europe increased, adding more Italians, Russians, Lithuanians, Czechs, and Poles. There had been some migration into the region from Eastern Europe prior to this, notably from Poland after the revolution of 1830, but the really large-scale movement from these areas began after the outbreak of anti-semitism in Russia in the early 1880s and continued through the 1890s. In 1921, the passing of an emergency immigration restriction law introduced a quota system, effectively choking off the influx from everywhere except northern and western Europe. This paved the way for the National Origins Act of 1924 which consolidated the policy of curtailed immigration. In spite of these restrictions immigration has continued to be important and special exceptions have been made in the case of German Jews, Hungarians, and Cubans.

More significant for Chicago and many other American cities has been the internal migration of Americans from the poorer southern states. Most of these have been Black, though significant numbers of southern whites, Spanish Americans, Mexicans, and

[13] As Thernstrom points out, the growth of smaller cities, even in the nineteenth century, was just as dramatic as the growth of such giants as Chicago, Pittsburgh, New York, or St. Louis. See S. Thernstrom, *Poverty and Progress* (Cambridge, Mass.: Harvard University Press, 1964), p. 9.

[14] It is estimated that one-fifth of all American families change their residence each year, and in urban slum areas the rate of movement is much higher. See *Americans at Mid-decade*, U.S. Department of Commerce, Series P-23, No. 16 (March 1966).

[15] See Pierre de Vise, *Chicago's Widening Color Gap*, Interuniversity Social Research Committee (Chicago: 1967), Report No. 2.

Puerto Ricans have also moved into the city. Chicago's Black population rose from two percent of the whole in 1910 to 32.7 percent in 1970.[16]

As these latest immigrants have moved in, many of the longer established residents have moved out—first to the outer fringes of the city itself and then increasingly to the suburbs, leaving core areas of low quality or deteriorating housing occupied by low income residents who are served by inferior schools, inadequate medical care, and overcrowded recreational facilities.

It has often been argued that this is part of a general process of social mobility in America whereby poor, badly educated and relatively unskilled people come from outside, settle in the inner city near to available work, gradually take advantage of the opportunities for advancement offered by American society, improve themselves and their children, and then move up in the social scale and out into better residential neighborhoods. It is popularly supposed that this is a peculiarly American process producing a culturally homogeneous and prosperous "middle class." The facts are somewhat different, and it is important to realize how and why they differ from this idealized picture, especially if we are to understand some of the variations in kinship and family norms which appear to obtain between ethnic groups.

The most obvious fact is that the Black population of Chicago is effectively confined to a few densely populated sections of the city because of the racially segregated market for housing. This in turn leads to segregated schools, churches, and other forms of social life. While the cores of these areas have remained solidly Black for many years, the peripheries have been expanding outward, particularly in the 1950s and 1960s. Certain aspects of this expansion are extremely interesting and throw light on the general social structure of the Chicago metropolitan area.[17]

At the risk of considerable oversimplification, one can say that

---

[16] U.S. Bureau of the Census, *Statistical Abstract of the United States: 1971* (92nd edition), Washington, D.C., 1971, p. 21.

[17] See de Vise, *Chicago's Widening Color Gap*, for a fuller discussion of the trends outlined here.

the Black areas in the city have tended to expand into adjacent areas of formerly relatively high status housing occupied by higher income populations of predominantly northwestern European stock (German, Scandinavian, Irish, and British). Their expansion has been resisted, and frequently blocked, in those contiguous areas occupied by lower income people of predominantly Polish, Czech, Italian, and Russian origin, who live in more modest houses and are less able to move out into higher cost suburban houses farther away from their work places. One notable exception to this generalization is the case of the Jews of Polish and Russian origin, who have tended to relocate in much the same way as the northwest Europeans.

While geographical mobility is often associated with occupational and status mobility, this is not always the case, and even where it is, the actual extent of mobility may not be great. The income and level of living of *all* residents of the Chicago metropolitan area has increased substantially over the past 20 years. The median family income for the whole Chicago area increased from $4,063 in 1950 to $9,400 in 1966, but this is not an across-the-board increase affecting all families equally. While all families gained something, the rich gained much more than the poor. The median family income in Chicago's ten richest communities rose from $7,390 in 1950 to $22,330 in 1966, while that of the ten poorest communities rose from $2,494 in 1950 to $4,809 in 1966. Measured against the average income for the whole metropolitan area, the median income in the poor areas *fell* from 61 percent to 51 percent of the average, while that of the richest areas rose from 182 percent to 238 percent. Much of the movement from city to suburbs was from the middle income group of whites, whose rise in real income was smaller than that of the high income group, and whose geographical mobility involved only limited status or occupational mobility.

The ten poorest communities in Chicago are all Black. In 1966 less than 10 percent of the population of all these areas taken together was white, and that proportion has probably declined since then. Within these areas one finds high unemployment rates, large numbers of persons on public assistance, high concentrations of public housing projects, high population densities, poor schools, inadequate medical services, and run-down shopping facilities. Income per family is low, but even more interesting is the tendency for families in these areas to depend upon more than one wage earner—a situation not commonly found in high and medium income areas. Black families with two earners still have a lower average aggregate income than one-earner white families. It is in relation to this fact that one should appreciate such misleading statements as that of D. P. Moynihan that the "family income" of young married Black couples is almost the same as that of whites.[18]

The pattern of population movement, education, and occupational mobility of immigrants, the persisting patterns of ethnic differentiation, and the continuing residential discrimination against nonwhites are all intimately related to the structure, growth, and changing technological base of the economic system. It would not be possible to discuss this in detail, particularly since there is a marked deficiency in statistical information regarding urban economic activity,[19] but the broad outline is fairly simple.

Chicago's early growth was stimulated by the opening up of the middle west as a great agricultural area. The city became the collection center for farm products, the hub of a mighty network of rail communications, and the center of manufacture and distribution to the new agricultural heartland. McCormick's tractor and farm machinery factories, Pullman's rail-car works, the stockyards, meat-packing plants, the grain storage areas of the city dockside, and the mail order supply houses of Sears and Montgomery Ward were all part of this pattern of development and economic expansion. The steel industry became another major component of local industrial development, while World War II saw the beginning of increasing growth of such new industries as light engineering and electronics.

[18] Memorandum to President Nixon, printed in *The New York Times*, Sunday, March 1, 1970. This is the remarkable document in which Moynihan advocates "benign neglect."

[19] See Doris B. Holleb, *Social and Economic Information for Urban Planning* (Chicago: Center for Urban Studies, University of Chicago, 1969), p. 98.

The relationship of immigrants, ethnic groups, and socially mobile individuals to the occupational structure is basic to their social experience and does much to determine many of the characteristics of their life styles and cultural conceptions.

Immigrants into the United States were employed in a wide range of industries, but generally moved first into those areas of the cities where work was available. Before the development of mass transportation and widespread ownership of automobiles, workers' residences were of necessity close to the place of employment. Even today a surprising number of city dwellers walk to work.[20] The bulk of employment offered to Chicago immigrants was unskilled, poorly paid, and dirty. Work was available in the stockyards, meat-packing plants, steel mills, on the railroads, in the building trades, in road, canal, and sewer building and other forms of general laboring, or in lowly paid service trades. As immigrants and their children became adjusted to American conditions, and as the children improved their educational levels, they were able to take advantage of such opportunities as presented themselves. These opportunities were most definitely not unlimited. The already established groups defended their status interests by excluding newcomers from their communities and social organizations, and by restricting access to the more desirable forms of employment.

Three sets of circumstances operated to render the situation more fluid than it might have been, and to keep open some entry into the broad category of "native American." One was the "democratic" nature of the political system which, despite its shortcomings, made every ethnic group count for *something* in the political arena, and also enabled some individuals to advance through employment in various governmental bureaucracies. Second, there was continuous economic growth accompanied by an increasing eleva-

---

[20] John F. Kain, "Urban Travel Behavior," in Leo F. Schnore and Henry Fagin (eds.), *Urban Research and Policy Planning* (Beverly Hills, California: Sage Publications Inc., 1967). He cites the 1960 census as reporting that 10 percent of all employed residents of urban areas walk to work. Only 10.9 percent use a bus or streetcar.

tion in the level of skills within most industries. Third, and most important, was the growth of trade unions and the establishment of broad criteria by which the rights of workers could be defined and protected. Before these instrumentalities of adjustment could come into play (attended by much violence and corruption), there was a period in the experience of most immigrant groups that was perceived by contemporaries as being disorganized, chaotic, and immoral. The massive documentation of the adjustments of Polish immigrants provided by Thomas and Znaniecki is replete with instances.[21] Religious and cultural organizations among Poles in Chicago were primarily mutual aid societies, though they grew around organizations and symbols transplanted from Poland. Although there has been a continuing core of organizations attempting to maintain the idea of a Polish nation within the American nation, Polish ethnic solidarity was originally a means of survival in a new and dangerous environment.[22]

The same general processes had operated in the case of the Irish, and are being repeated with Afro-Americans and Spanish Americans. However, racism now intervenes as an additional complicating variable which, most clearly in the case of Afro-Americans, makes it impossible to treat the latter simply as "ethnic" groups.

We see, then, a complex process whereby American cities like the Chicago metropolitan area have grown into huge industrial–residential centers with an elaborate division of labor, and an equally elaborate differentiation of residential neighborhoods. These residential areas tend to be class or income homogeneous except where a continuing sense of ethnic identity, or an enforced racial homogeneity, have accommodated more economically diverse populations.

The direct experience of our field research was that, while consciousness of ethnic identity persists at all levels of society, it is

[21] William I. Thomas and Florian Znaniecki, *The Polish Peasant in Europe and America* (Boston: Richard A. Badger, The Goreham Press, 1918).

[22] See Upton Sinclair, *The Jungle* (New York: Doubleday & Company, Inc., 1906), for a vivid fictional account of Chicago at the turn of the century.

of rapidly decreasing significance as a factor affecting the behavior of those who are middle class. In fact, one aspect of becoming middle class is the abandonment of most of the behavioral characteristics of ethnicity, a process considerably aided by orientation toward individual achievement, the rational control of events and things, and looking to the future rather than to the past. These values are not simply abstractly held cultural symbols; they are the counterpart of the middle-class individual's life experience of self-transformation through school and college, his involvement in a career situation which demands a constant search for success and promotion, and his movement into a bureaucratically-ordered world in which ethnic identity is of negligible significance.[23]

For the lower class, "ethnicity," or a particularistic identification of some kind, seems to be an intrinsic part of the structuring of group and intergroup relations. Such identification runs the gamut from traditional distinctions among such European groups as Italians, Poles, and Lithuanians, to primarily racial distinctions, as in the case of Blacks and American Indians, American regional groups such as "Appalachian Whites," and groups which are both culturally and racially defined, such as Mexican–Americans or Chinese–Americans. The clustering of lower-class people into ethnic areas is partly a function of the migratory process itself, and is as common in West African cities as in Chicago, but it is also a means for maximizing security within a difficult and unpredictable world. The segmentation of lower-class areas into ethnic groups must also be seen as a social process which may continue despite a diminution in actual cultural differences.[24]

Most of the dirty, difficult, and degrading occupations into which European immigrants came have been transformed by technological advance, spurred on by political and trade union action,

---

[23] There are obvious exceptions to such a generalization. As Moynihan and Glazer show, there can be considerable ethnic concentration even in higher status employment, and there is often a sense that certain industries are the preserve of certain ethnic groups. See Nathan Glazer and Daniel P. Moynihan, *Beyond the Melting Pot* (Cambridge, Mass.: M.I.T. Press, 1963).

[24] See Frederick Barth, *Ethnic Groups and Boundaries* (London: George Allen & Unwin, 1969).

so that the present-day labor force is more skilled, more adept at the use of machinery, and more educated. Roads and sewers are no longer built with pick and shovel. Although the construction industry still uses much casual and unskilled labor, the complexity of building technology demands more skilled specialists than ever. Whole new industries have developed, such as the automobile industry, with production techniques which demand little skill but sustain high rates of pay for those employed on assembly lines. Dirty, difficult, and degrading work has not disappeared, but important changes have taken place in the nature of work and its symbolic significance to status.

If the sweatshops, factories, and labor sites which exploited the cheap labor of the European immigrants have been transformed, the question is: What has become of the "lower class"?

There are several ways to answer such a question. In terms of specific groups and individuals, one can say that much of the old lower class has been transformed into the modern working class, considerably upgraded in skill, better paid and better educated, but still exhibiting many of the cultural orientations of their parents and grandparents. In terms of the structure of the economy and the persistence of poorly paid and low prestige jobs, it is evident that there has been considerable continuity despite technological change and the progressive upgrading of industrial work. Particularly in the service occupations there is noticeable continuity of structure, but drastic change in personnel. Cleaning women, janitors, dishwashers, hospital workers, garbage truck workers, streetcleaners, and unskilled workers of all kinds are likely to be Black, Puerto Rican, or white immigrants from the rural south. Such persons are frequently filling the positions which have always been filled by recent immigrants, but there is the additional factor of racial discrimination which constitutes a brake upon the upward mobility of those defined as nonwhite. Finally, one must consider that component of the lower class which has also been highly persistent despite changes in personnel: the unemployed, chronic welfare cases, petty criminals, alcoholics, drug addicts, and so on. In a society dominated by the values of the affluent middle class there is always a tendency to characterize the whole of the lower class in terms of this unfortunate, deviant or disorganized component. While it is true that the general economic insecurity of lower-class life makes unemployment and welfare dependency an ever-present possibility, and petty crime, drunkenness, and drug addiction a familiar experience, this does not exhaust or typify the description of lower-class life styles.

The lower class, then, can be characterized in either of two ways. First, it can be viewed in terms of occupation, with its center of gravity in the lower reaches of the new working class, filling positions in which there is little orientation to or possibility of promotion beyond the skilled craftsman level. Second, it can be characterized in terms of a general cultural orientation which stresses security, traditional attitudes to authority, and involvement in particularistic relationships springing from local community ethnic and kinship ties.

Black Culture and the African Heritage

One important issue that must be dealt with before concluding this chapter is the question of the extent of variation in "lower-class cultural orientations" among ethnic and racial groups. It could be objected that much of our discussion of lower-class family structure is really a discussion of Afro-Americans and therefore does not apply to the white working class, for example. It must be said that a significant portion of our data does pertain to lower-class Black families, but we have data on lower-class white families as well, and are confident that our generalizations have wider application.

There *are* differences in expression, taste and stylistic preference among American ethnic groups. The persistence of languages, food preferences, specific churches, musical styles and other elements all testify to the importance of ethnic differences, but these differences seem important mainly as identity and boundary markers, rather than constituting the fundamental basis of a culture which is sharply differentiated by ethnic group affiliation. Most immigrants to the northern cities of the United States came from lower status groups, usually with an agrarian background. This is equally true whether they came from Ireland, Poland, Roumania, Mississippi, West Virginia, or Mexico. Some of the later Jewish immigration is an exception in that it involved people from European cities, and of course there has always been a small proportion of immigrants of higher status with higher education. Nonetheless, we maintain the validity of the general point that much "ethnic life-style" is of rural, traditional, lower status origin, and the process of becoming a middle-class American necessarily involves abandonment of much of the class orientation of ethnic life ways, no matter how much retention there is of formal allegiance to a general ethnic identity.

It would appear that ethnicity may serve to segment the lower class into distinguishable communities with a degree of differentiation, but the very traditionalism, rural origin, and adjustive functions of these subunits provides a certain structural uniformity which coincides with and reinforces the general lower-class orientation derived from similar positions in the occupational, power, and prestige hierarchy of American society. (Ethnicity among the middle class is much less significant, and even when it is symbolically emphasized it has little distinctive social content.)[25] Given the existence of such structural uniformity, it seems equally clear that there will be some residual effect exercised by the *specific* cultural tradition of which ethnic groups are the bearers.

[25] See David M. Schneider, *American Kinship: A Cultural Account* (Englewood Cliffs, N.J.: Prentice-Hall, Inc., 1968), Chap. VI. Ironically, it is middle-class Blacks who are forced by institutionalized racism into a common awareness of their common history and common situation, and who therefore are forced to act as a part of a more inclusive Black "ethnic group."

MIDDLE-CLASS AND LOWER-CLASS KINSHIP: CONTRASTING FEATURES

Chapter 4

The complex nature of modern American society (lightly touched upon in Chapter 3) provides the context within which the differentiation of kinship and familial role structures has developed. In this chapter we shall limit ourselves to the presentation of simple models which bring into sharp relief certain clusters of features that we wish to contrast. The subtle gradations of empirical variation are ignored, and it is clear from our previous discussion of this subject that a simple contrast between "middle" and "lower" class can only be a very rough approximation to the understanding of the factors producing such variation.

A considerable body of writing has developed around the idea of the "mother-centered" nature of lower-class family relations. Much of this is specific to certain ethnic groups, notably Blacks and American Indians, but there is also enough written on white families to make this a factor to be considered. Two of the best discussions come from England; Young and Wilmott reported the "Mum"–focused pattern of kinship ties in East London in the 1950s, and Elizabeth Bott emphasized the link between this pattern and the high level of female solidarity in residentially stable neighborhoods.[1] In neither of these studies was there an attempt to

[1] Michael Young and Peter Wilmott, *Family and Kinship in East London* (London: Routledge & Kegan Paul Ltd., 1957); Elizabeth Bott, *Family and Social Network* (London: Tavistock Publications Ltd., 1957).

link the pattern of solidarity of females, and of mother and children, to the occurrence of female-headed households. Indeed, the incidence of female-headed households is not unusually high in English lower-class communities.

We have argued that a kinship system is a system of solidary relations at the normative level. However, it is clear that there are priorities and subsolidarities within the whole span of the kinship universe. Informants speak of distant relatives to whom they may feel little attachment, just as they speak of close relatives and immediate family. It is thus possible to identify a hierarchy of solidary bonds, irrespective of the actual content of those bonds in a particular system. This is nicely expressed (somewhat negatively) by a children's play-song recorded in the British Isles:

> You canna shove yer Granny off a bus,
> No you canny shove yer Granny off a bus,
> No you canna shove yer Granny
> For she's your mammy's mammy.
> No you canny shove yer granny off a bus.
>
> You can shove yer other granny off a bus,
> You can shove yer other granny off a bus.
> You can shove yer other granny
> For she's yer father's mammy.
> You can shove yer other granny off a bus.

That particular distinction between mother's mother and father's mother is not a formal distinction within the structure of the kinship system. It arises at the normative, or role structure, level because nonkinship elements enter into the definition of those roles. The frequent contact and mutual identification of mother and daughter in their activities as women and as child-rearers results in a sense of particular closeness, especially if they live near to, or with, each other. Such a close relationship may arise from unique circumstances in a particular case, but a pattern of priority of solidarity may become normal in a given society or group within a society. It is our contention that there is some variation between classes in the definition of the boundaries of "immediate family," and that this is associated with a variation in *the pattern of priority of solidary emphasis* within the central core of the kinship system. In one sense all relatives are the proper focus of relations of diffuse enduring solidarity, but relatives are differentiated by sex, age, occupation, and many other criteria, over and above their pure kinship status, and it is these other factors that lead to variation in solidarity patterns.

We believe that there are marked contrasts which can be expressed initially in terms of a gross distinction between a middle-class and a lower-class pattern. A simple sorting of the data of observation cannot yield two such discrete categories; this is a first approximation to an understanding of the dynamics of these variations. This method of contrasting abstract models is chosen over the alternative of trying to identify "subcultures" precisely because we wish to avoid *premature* freezing of variables into such empirical clusters.

Whereas the middle class lays strong emphasis upon the self-sufficiency and solidarity of the nuclear family against all other kinship ties and groupings, the lower class (whatever its household group structure may be) does not emphasize nuclear family self-sufficiency. On the contrary, the emphasis is on help, cooperation, and solidarity with a wide range of kin. This is not to say that there is a stress on "the extended family," or that there are clearly structured kinship groups of wide span; the emphasis is upon keeping open the options—upon maximizing the number of relationships which involve diffuse solidarity. It is for this reason that one finds a tendency to *create* kinship ties out of relationships which are originally ties of friendship. For example, we found the category "play-kin" to be important for many of our lower-class Black informants. These are individuals who are "just like" a mother, sister, brother, aunt, uncle, or, less frequently, some other category of kinsman. Liebow has described the phenomenon of "going for brothers" among lower-class Black men in Washington.[2] Apart from this kind of semiformalized relationship, lower-class persons

---

[2] Elliot Liebow, *Tally's Corner* (Boston, Little, Brown & Co., 1967).

develop close and intimate bonds of friendship, particularly with persons of the same sex who are frequently described as being very close, "like a member of my family."

There is a sense in which the middle-class pattern of nuclear family solidarity is undifferentiated; everyone must work together for the good and betterment of all.[3] But the family has a life span. It starts with the marriage of a man and woman, proceeds through procreation and the raising of children who grow up and leave home to found their own families, leaving the parents together until one or both die. Of necessity the top priority concerning solidarity must be that of husband and wife, who become mother and father, but must also continue to be husband and wife "until death do them part." They are the solid core around which the whole system revolves; they are the beginning and the end. If one of them long survives the other, he or she becomes a problem, as myriad nursing homes and retirement colonies testify. Although mother and children constitute a most important focus of solidary relations, it is felt to be wrong to sacrifice the relationship of husband and wife to the demands of children. Husband, wife, son, and daughter all pull together, go out together, take vacations together, do things together at home—but it is known that the children will grow up and leave home, while husband and wife have a permanent life together.

The lower-class pattern places the primary stress elsewhere— upon the solidarity of mother and children—while it stresses the separateness of men and women.

Although our primary concern here is with the shape and internal ordering of the immediate family, these differences affect the patterning of wider kinship ties. Briefly, the outcome of the middle-class pattern is what might be called a "chain kindred"; that is, a structure something like a charm bracelet, in that a series of families are linked together through the sibling bond or the parent-child

---

[3] Of course the cultural value stress upon individualism is a constant factor at all class levels and penetrates to the very core of kinship units, so that the emphasis upon family solidarity is also seen as serving the end of facilitating individuality.

bond, but with the nuclear family as the fundamental unit.[4] The outcome of the lower-class pattern of solidary emphasis is a reticulated pattern of person-to-person ties. It may not be a perfectly uniform network, for there will be both bunching and unevenness of mesh, but there is an openness of pattern which contrasts with the middle-class emphasis on closed nuclear family units. One also sees a tendency for a collection of kin often referred to as "close family" to be important in both solidary and interactive terms, and to be different from the household group. Gans has noted the same phenomenon for Italian Americans.[5]

Having sketched the contrast in these rather stark outlines, let us now add some detail.

Middle-Class Kinship Patterns

In middle-class American kinship, husband and wife are supposed to make a single unit, to share and share alike. They are jointly responsible for the family and its fate, for the children and their future. The family should live together in a home of its own, apart from others, even other kinsmen. They should have their own bedroom, kitchen, and bathroom. This place, with its physical separation from other places and other people, stands for the autonomy and independence of the family. Indeed, just as membership in the family is not shared with the parents of either spouse, so, too, occupation of the home—a house, apartment, or whatever form the quarters take—is not ideally shared with the parents of either spouse. By the same token, when the children grow up, are married, and have families of their own, the independence of their family will be marked by separate homes.[6]

---

[4] This can be seen, though not always with perfect consistency, when collecting a "spontaneous listing" prior to taking a genealogy. The informant is asked to list his kin and the list tends, in the case of the middle-class informant, to be given in terms of nuclear family clusters.

[5] Herbert Gans, *The Urban Villagers* (New York: The Free Press, 1962).

[6] Some of the general structural features set out here were remarked upon by Parsons in his essay, "The Kinship System of the Contemporary United States"

The unity of husband and wife in middle-class American kinship is not altered by the fact that their roles are differentiated. Indeed, such differentiation is in large measure defined with reference to the unity of the family, maintenance of the family as a whole, and the future of the family, especially the children. This future orientation is a very important part of the organization of the middle-class American family.

The husband/father should earn the family's "living." His job, his occupation, should provide for the family's food, clothing, shelter, and other material needs.

It is the wife/mother who is responsible for the home and for the care of the children, particularly in their early years. This does not mean that she must not hold a job or what is sometimes called "go out to work." Rather, if she does go out to work, it can be only when the home and care of children and similar problems are under control.

It is not really very easy to distinguish the degree of solidarity between husband and wife from that between parent and child in middle-class American kinship, and this is in itself an important statement about the structure of the priorities. For the family as a unit seems to take a kind of precedence over any particular combination of its constituent members. Ideally, the aims and ends and goals of the family and the roles of its members are so orchestrated that the well-being, happiness, and obligations of any member are coordinated with those of the family as a whole. Therefore, it does not make much sense to see the nuclear family as an array of dyadic relationships as against a total configuration.

There is, however, one special point where the primacy of the conjugal bond in middle-class American kinship is clearly demonstrated. This is the point of separation of children from parents, when children marry and found families of their own. Just as the parents left their parents' home to found a home of their own, so too

---

(1943), reprinted in Talcott Parsons, *Essays in Sociological Theory* (Glencoe, Illinois: The Free Press, 1949). Interesting and comparable data are to be found in John Seeley, Alexander Sim and Elizabeth W. Loosley, *Crestwood Heights: A Study of the Culture of Suburban Life* (New York: Basic Books Inc., 1956).

their children will "grow up," marry and found families of their own. This is not a mere physical separation; rather, the physical separation marks an array of different aspects of the independence of grown children from their parents.

We have spoken here of "parent" and "child" and "spouse." These kinship terms disregard the difference in sex between parents, between children, and between spouses. They have been chosen precisely because sex difference is *not* a significant difference in the pattern of solidary emphasis in middle-class American kinship. The contents of the bonds between mother and son, mother and daughter, father and son, father and daughter are defined differently. But the priority on the solidarity is the same for mother–son as it is for mother–daughter, the same for father–son as it is for father–daughter. And so too siblings; the normatively defined strength of the solidary bond is the same for brothers as for sisters as for brother and sister.

Next, let us consider the question of authority. In middle-class American kinship, authority properly resides in reason, rationality, technical know-how, the best expertise available. It is not defined as inherent in or an inalienable attribute of any particular kind of relative, such as a mother or a father, a husband or a wife. It may happen that husbands often know more about certain things than wives do, and therefore tend to make certain decisions more often. But the grounds for the decision rest on knowledge and judgment, not on the husband's automatic right. The fundamental question when problems arise, decisions must be taken, or choices made, is that of the wisest, most reasonable, best, or proper course to follow, and reason is the ultimate authority. The question is, "What is the right thing to do?" What is the sensible thing to do?," and *not* "Who has the right to make the decision?" Ideally, decisions are made collectively and in terms of rational choices rationally arrived at.

The use and maintenance of household machinery is a good example. There is a presumption that men are more mechanically inclined and have greater brawn and muscle than women. Yet when it comes to the question of what to do about certain kinds of household machinery that break down, the decision concerns how to deal with it best. Women may use the machines daily, and know their neuroses and just how to cope with them. Hence, whatever the mechanical aptitude of men, if a woman knows how to fix the washing machine better than her husband, she does so, without standing on traditional rights invested in one sex or the other. Alternatively, and more frequently, she will simply go ahead and call in a repairman, dealing with him directly and competently without her husband's mediation.

Children, school, and similar matters are like household machinery in this regard. The primary question is, "What is the best thing to do under the circumstances?" "What is the effective course of action toward the given goal?" If an expert is the best person to ask for help in solving such a problem, and there are no financial obstacles, then the expert may be appealed to precisely on the ground that he ought to know, not because he has a traditional right. This is why pediatricians, psychiatrists, and guidance counselors are able to earn a living.[7]

The idea that father is the head of the family and can behave like some oriental despot is a fantasy which some fathers have, but this is certainly not the normative definition of how authority is properly distributed or exercised. If "father knows best," it is in his knowledge and wisdom that his authority resides. Father should play a representative role between the family and the outside world, dealing with the tax authorities, the real estate board, the neighborhood property owners association where he knows what he is doing. But that he has the right to issue orders and have them promptly obeyed (if it ever was true) is a thing of the past so far as the formal norms of urban middle-class American kinship are concerned.[8]

---

[7] See the work on a Canadian middle-class suburb by Seeley, Sim, and Loosley, *Crestwood Heights*, for a very interesting discussion of the use of "experts" of this kind.

[8] The idea of the middle-class husband–father as a minor autocrat within his domestic circle was common in Europe and was not unknown in America. It was linked to a time when there was much sharper sex-role differentiation, when husband–fathers may well have been head of a family enterprise, and when inheritance and continuity of a family line were stressed. In this respect the changes toward a *modern* middle-class pattern are profound.

It is thus, for the middle class, not a question of who has the right to exercise authority, but rather who knows how: who knows how to make the paycheck stretch, to cover costs, to plan a vacation, to discipline children, to talk with the teacher, to fix the furnace, and so on. The attribution of authority more to reason than to persons in middle-class American kinship is closely related to the stress on independence mentioned earlier. One aspect of this is that, for the spouses, interdependence on each other is the highest value, while independence from other persons outside the family is its complement. Thus, when the middle-class wife bears a child, it may be taken as a mark of incompetence on her husband's part or disloyalty on hers if she has to bring in her mother to help with the new baby and the running of the home. The wife should be able to depend on her husband for whatever help she needs. The general proposition seems to be that the family ought to be able to stand on its own feet; it should not need to depend on any outside resources for help.

This stress on independence also applies to the growing child. He should be able to adjust to and master his environment and learn to use it for his own ends. He should go to school and do well there, for he will need those skills later when he goes to work and founds his own family. Training the child to independence, self-reliance, and competence is an important task which middle-class families are supposed to undertake with the greatest seriousness and dedication, and by using such rational guides and experts as may be necessary.

It is in this light that we can understand the seemingly senseless and radical shifts in fads of child-rearing which have beset the middle class for the past 50 years or so. It is not merely that the experts have changed their minds with unpredictable rapidity. It is also that the American middle-class family is supposed to be guided by rational, reasonable, scientific considerations, and when these turn out to be unstable, all the family can do is to stay with the experts however much they change around. At one period, strict scheduling of feeding, sleeping, and playing dominated the nursery. This was followed by a period of what appeared to some unsympathetic observers to be almost chaotic permissiveness, with feeding on demand, toilet training "when the child was ready and initiated it himself," play when the spirit moved him, and of course aggressive impulses were not sharply suppressed. Both extreme permissiveness and strict scheduling were aimed at precisely the same end: the independence, autonomy, self-reliance, and competence of the growing child and of the adult he was to become. It was believed that this could be achieved by rational means, particularly with the help of experts.

A special problem of independence training is that of "impulse control." For the child, this consists of control over his sphincters and over his aggressive, destructive, and sexual impulses. The central problem of impulse control in middle-class child training is to teach the child the proper ways, times, places, aims and objects for these impulses. The aim is *control*, or self-discipline, that is, control guided by rational considerations taken with reference to accepted goals. It is not that aggression or sexuality are in themselves either good or bad, it is that the individual must be able to do things in the right way, at the right time, and *he* must manage his impulses and not let them manage him. The rule of reason is the dominant value; the particular impulse is defined as problematic, but there is no strong positive or negative value attached to the particular impulse per se. Instead, the positive value is attached to self-discipline, control, and the rational application of means to ends. Self-indulgence in opening sphincters, or venting aggressive or sexual impulses purely for gratification, is disvalued, at least in part, because such self-indulgence implies a lack of self-control or self-discipline and is likely to be counterproductive in the attainment of goals defined as acceptable and valued.

The primacy of independence and of rational control over action, especially over impulses, is most clearly visible in relation to work and job and the occupational sphere. The highest rewards are paid for competence, for doing a job well, for being successful in one's occupation. This phrasing, or definition of the situation, is applied to the family and to kinship roles as well. The question is put, "How good a job does he do as a father?" or "She is not doing her job as a mother" or "He's incompetent as a husband." For the middle class, there are standards of performance which are applied to kinship and family roles as there are to occupational roles, and judgments and evaluations are made in terms of those standards of competence. These standards are most prominent for the role of the husband/father. The man who cannot get work and hold it and maintain his family according to the standards of his class, who is unable to provide for his wife and children, is a man who has failed as a father, a husband, and a worker.

Standards of competence apply equally, though perhaps not quite so conspicuously, to women as wives and mothers. A middle-class woman who is a slovenly housekeeper is not held in high regard. Indeed, it may be said that she should be "ashamed of herself." But a woman who can manage a large house, a large number of children, a station wagon or two, and a church club, who can live an active social life and be a good hostess for her rising young executive husband—know whom to flirt with among his superiors and just how much—such a woman may be admired and approved of by her middle-class friends and neighbors, for she is competent at her job as wife and mother. The ability to manage such tasks and manage them well is highly valued.

Rationality, self-control, self-discipline, independence, and the ability to do a job well are all aspects of the autonomy of the individual, the competence of the person. These are attributes of the actor, they are not seen as, or defined as, functions of external imperatives which enforce behavior. It is certainly true that if the person does not behave according to certain standards, sanctions are applied, and there are not only standards to guide behavior, but also punishments of various kinds for failing to conform. Within certain very wide limits, these sanctions are largely in the form of failure to achieve what are defined as possible rewards. That is, the failure of impulse control within certain limits does not necessarily send one to jail or bring down the force of the law. Rather, the punishment consists in "failure," of being a failure in not reaching objectives, of not getting ahead, and being unable to maintain one's hoped-for place in society.

These are individual matters, attributes of the person, aspects of the self. In these terms are expressed the idea of being the master of one's fate. It is up to the individual to control himself; it is his responsibility to do what he ought to do.

So too a person's identity as a man or a woman is closely bound up with his competence and success at a job. This is true whether it be a man's occupation or a woman's position as wife/mother. Competence and success at these jobs are identified very closely with being "a man" or with being "a woman." "What kind of man are you that you cannot earn a living and support your wife and children?" is the sort of question that is asked from time to time, and the very question which many men had put to them or which they asked themselves during the great depression of the 1930s. For the middle-class American man, sexual potency is intimately associated with, and often expressed through, occupational competence and success.

American culture postulates a separation of the person from certain of his goals. The postulation holds that the person's relationship to those goals is problematic, and the problematic element is the person himself. If he works hard, if he uses his head, if he tries, he has every right to expect to reach those goals. But the onus is on the person; it is, as the cliché has it, "up to him." Hard work guided by rational considerations ought to be productive, and it is in doing something that gets done, in making some thing useful, that hard work becomes productive.

These are all conditions which inform the cultural definitions of kinsmen as persons, or the norms of social action, in middle-class American society. The man in the family should earn a good living and he should do this by hard work. He should be able to support his family. His wife should do a good job of being a wife and a mother. His children should learn that hard work is its own reward, even though other rewards may be expected as well. They should know that you don't get things by crying, cheating, stealing, or lying, but that if you try hard and work hard and use your intelligence, then you *can* have the things you want. Everyone has to learn to stand on his own feet, to be independent of his mother and father, to love his family as the family loves him, but to make his own way in life and to start his own family. If this sounds like a string of clichés, the reason is simple: it *is* a string of clichés through which these truths held to be self-evident are expressed over and over again.

We turn now to sex and sexuality, and consider the place which is structurally defined for it in middle-class American kinship. One of the parents' tasks is to teach the child impulse control, of which sexual impulses are obviously important. We have noted that it is not sexual activity as such that is held to be wrong, evil, or immoral, but rather its uncontrolled expression at the wrong time, the wrong place, or with the wrong person.

Illegitimacy is held to be immoral and wrong by middle-class Americans, and its wrongness resides in many different things. The child has no family, its position at law is problematic, its paternity and therefore its proper claim on its father may be in doubt, and so on. These and other similar, practical, rational problems which arise all relate to the normative definition of what constitutes a "family." The illegitimate child also reflects on the failure of impulse control by its biological parents, and this may be what provokes such emotional hostility to the idea of illegitimacy. A girl allowing herself to be seduced, a boy stooping low enough to seduce her, these are shameful acts in themselves. No amount of the expression of romantic love can obscure their actions; indeed, to say that the child was the result of overwhelming love is only to concede the loss of impulse control.

It would be wrong to interpret this as an indication of abhorrence for sex. Coitus and erotic activity are good, healthy, proper, and expected parts of marriage. Sexual relations are a very important part of the husband–wife relationship, for they not only express love, but they are, in essence, *the* culturally prescribed bond between husband and wife. A marriage which has not been consummated is not a marriage. Like everything else in the middle class, the norms of middle-class American kinship hold that action should be guided by the right, the reasonable, and the rational, and so a constant search for these goes on, not only where the treatment and cure of disease is concerned, but in the management of financial resources, the preparation of meals, and also in the conduct of sexual intercourse. It is interesting to speculate as to whether there are as many "how to do it" books on sexual intercourse as there are on child-rearing and child care, or just who is Doctor Spock's counterpart in the field of coitus. In any event, the guiding principle is the same in both of these areas. The success of the studies by Masters and Johnson is indicative of the trend. It is the search for the rational guide and the quest for the expert to provide it. One more element is evident, and that is the very high value placed on work. Simply to experience gratification is questionable, if not actually immoral, but to work hard for a just reward (using the best professional advice available), and to achieve it, is the acme of gratification—according to the standards of middle-class culture.[9]

Lower-Class Kinship Patterns

The normative structure of lower-class American kinship does not stress the independence and integrity of the unit of husband, wife, and children in the way we have outlined for the middle-class model. Starting from the same "pure" kinship elements and definitions, the normative system permits, and even enjoins, a more open pattern of solidary emphasis, which allows a good deal of elasticity in the boundary of households and of that group considered to be "close family." To put it another way, the composition of lower-class households can be more diverse without being considered unusual, there can be more coming and going on the part of those who live together, and ties maintained across household boundaries may be as intense as those between persons who live together. Despite this emphasis upon person-to-person relations (as opposed to some designated collectivity such as the nuclear family), there are solidary priorities. As we said at the beginning of this chapter, the primary solidarity is between mother and children, while the basic differentiation is between males and females. This is not to say that women

[9] See Lionel S. Lewis and Dennis Brissett, "Sex as Work: A Study of Avocational Counseling," *Social Problems,* 15, No. 1 (1967), pp. 8–17.

are not dependent upon males; males' earnings are an important part of the economic base of household groups. However, dependence is not structured in such a way that conjugal solidarity is at the apex of the whole familial normative system. Similarly, conjugal love is as basic an ingredient of lower-class kinship as it is for the middle class, but sexual relations are not loaded with the same symbolic meaning of "unity" because the symbols of sex also mean differentiation of a marked kind in the nonkinship domains.

Within the lower class, child-bearing and child care are unequivocally within the women's sphere of competence; men leave this to women, and are similarly not inclined to take part in the running of the domestic aspects of family life. Washing clothes, making beds, cleaning the house, cooking, and washing dishes are all women's work, and for men to interfere in these activities may appear to be effeminate as well as demeaning. The lower-class man will help out with such chores in case of emergency, such as a wife's sickness or absence, but he will probably do them badly; it would be quite acceptable, in fact preferable, to let another woman from outside take over these tasks. Just as there are jobs women can do best because they are "women's work," so are there men's jobs around the house. Fixing machinery, taking care of the furnace, maintaining the fabric of the house are all appropriate male tasks, and of course the maintenance and driving of automobiles is an area in which males excel and from which lower-class women may be specifically excluded, or under some circumstances, exclude themselves.

The relationship between mother and son is a focus of both solidarity and differentiation. Sons are expected to grow up and seek independence from their mother in a man's world, while at the same time maintaining a lifelong love and affection for her which may well involve considerable economic support. A man's gratitude and tender love is due his mother, and that love is separated from the sexual dominance he is supposed to display in relation to women who are sexual partners. What is common in a man's relationships to his mother and to his wife is the provision of support by the man and domestic services by the woman. The only significant difference is the wife's engagement in sexual relations, a fact which makes the epithet "motherfucker" such a powerful and meaningful symbol.

Mother and daughter have the same kind of relationship as mother and son, except that it is reinforced by their identity as women and therefore has even greater solidary emphasis than the mother–son bond, especially when both sons and daughters have grown up. The identification and closeness of mother and daughter may be expressed in many ways. They may live in the same house, or live close enough to each other to visit back and forth all the time. If they are not close enough to see each other every day, they may telephone frequently. Telephone communication of this kind is also common between middle-class mothers and daughters; the lower-class pattern is not the existence of such a solidary bond, but its greater emphasis and the recognition that it does not necessarily conflict with a woman's relationship to her husband or boyfriend, which is thought to be of a quite different nature.

In the same way that mother and daughter are closer than mother and son, so sister and sister are closer than sister and brother. There is no equivalent identification of father and son, brother and brother. This is consistent with the fact that men are defined as more independent and autonomous than women; even when opportunities arise for cooperation, the independence of the male may be threatened by close interdependence. Men move out into varied occupations and a world of leisure time activity in which each individual finds friends of his own age.

While the middle-class family may spend much of its leisure together, this is not common in the lower class. The middle-class home may provide space for each individual to be alone, and space for the whole family to be together, whereas the lower-class home is likely to be excessively crowded. Each individual has to get out to be alone, or to do the things he or she wishes to do with his friends.

Authority in the lower-class family is not defined in the same way as we outlined for the middle class. Authority is vested in males because they are strong, dominating, and have a traditional right to make decisions. If not obeyed they can enforce their authority by physical chastisement. There is no process of careful consideration of all alternatives, each member making his views known and the final decision resting on a weighing of facts. In practice, views *are* made known by suggestion, cajolery, nagging, or assertion, but the decision is generally presented as arbitrary. Frequently, of course, there is no decision-making male available, and even when there is, it is by no means certain that the decisions are always his; the fact remains that lower-class norms set up males as the proper bearers of authority. If a woman proves stronger, tougher, or more dominating than the man who is around, the authority passes to her, but such an occurrence indicates that something is wrong. It is important not to confuse female decision making in appropriate domains with female dominance. Lower-class women may have a wide range of decision-making powers in relation to running the home and caring for children that gives a false impression of dominance. Two factors are important here: one is the marked segregation of sex-roles such that domestic functions are women's work, and the other is the structural separation of conjugal relations from child-rearing functions. The middle-class model fuses all these elements, whereas the lower-class model keeps them separate and capable of independent variation.

We said earlier that the middle-class family, in its search for the right, best, and most rational thing to do, will seek out the advice and help of a wide range of experts, from pediatricians and pedodontists to psychiatrists and writers of sex manuals. In recent years it has seemed that many members of the lower class similarly draw upon the services of such experts as caseworkers and counselors. The situation is very different. The lower-class world is one of uncertainty, a world which is uncontrollable, unpredictable, and apparently irrational. In such a world one must seek security, adapting to what cannot be avoided and attempting to maximize possible sources of help. The caseworker, the counselor, and the political party Ward Captain are all possible sources of help in time of greater adversity (at no time do things run entirely in the right direction). These sources are not thought of as being specialized or differentiated; they are merely another extension of a traditional network, capable of indefinite extension, of possible sources of help.

We saw that the training of the middle-class child places considerable emphasis upon independence and competence as attributes of the individual who should learn to control his impulses in order to attain goals which are deemed proper. It is not that impulses per se are improper, but their free expression may interfere with the individual's task of achieving his ends. For the lower class the emphasis is quite differently placed. The individual is taught submission rather than self-control, and in the process of child-rearing there is much less stress upon control of impulses as means to the achievement of individual ends. The growing child is expected to conform to traditional ways of doing things, taught to obey those in a position of authority, and positively sanctioned by physical punishment when necessary. It is in this light that one must view the lower-class woman's desire to have a man around the house to "discipline the children" lest they grow up "lawless." This lower class "authoritarianism" is less a specific feature of familial relationships than an aspect of general age-role and sex-role differentiation. Just as the aged are respected, taken care of, and deferred to (within limits), so the young are enjoined to show respect and obedience to adults simply because of the particularistic qualities which differentiate age groups. Obedience is exacted not by reasoning but by punishment, hence the frequent designation of lower-class parents as "authoritarian." Both classes display a similar attribution of responsibility to the *individual* for failure to live up to expectations, but whereas in the middle class it is deemed the individual's failure to master his impulses and to attain proper control of self in order to achieve laudable ends, for the lower class it is deemed to be a flaw in the very nature of the individual—"he turned out to be no good"—or an essentially uncontrollable concatenation of circumstances—"he never had good luck."

While it would seem that a difference of value emphasis is involved in these different orientations toward individual behavior, there is also a concomitant difference in the circumstances and facilities with which the two classes typically operate. Whereas the middle-class orientation is characterized by a preoccupation with planning, the lower-class person can seldom control circumstances to that extent, and tends to accept luck—good or bad—and make the most of it, devising ad hoc solutions to problems and savoring happiness to the full when it presents itself.

This is related to the fact that the lower class tends to place a high premium upon those qualities of the individual which enable him to manipulate circumstances and people, and somehow come out ahead. This requires style, fluent speech, quick wit, and extraordinary personality or innate warmth and "soul," rather than the qualities of self-discipline which enable the individual to achieve his ends through a long process of training and work. All lower-class groups, irrespective of ethnic origin, place emphasis upon these qualities of manipulation. Today the lower-class Afro-American is often taken as the epitome of lower classness, much as the Irishman was in another day. It has always appeared to the middle classes that the behavior of the lower class is lacking in self-control and is essentially immoral. Friedrich Engels, while castigating the industrial bourgeoisie for its inhuman treatment of the English working class, could also write that the drunkenness and sexual immorality of many English workers

> inevitably follows from the circumstances in which this class of society is placed. The workers have been left to themselves without the moral training necessary for the proper control of their sexual desires . . . all the failings of the workers may be traced to the same sort of origin—an unbridled thirst for pleasure, to lack of foresight, inability to adjust themselves to the discipline of the social order, and above all, the inability to sacrifice immediate pleasure for a future advantage.[10]

He did not point out the remarkable similarity in the tastes and activities of the English upper classes of the time!

The lower-class woman has always been depicted in the dual role of victim and victimizer. She is pictured as subjected to the abusive treatment of an irresponsible husband, forced to work herself to a premature old age in order to keep the home together,

---

[10] Friedrich Engels, *The Condition of the Working Class in England* (Stanford, Calif.: Stanford University Press, 1968), p. 144.

sacrificing everything for her children while her husband thinks only of his own pleasure and is not averse to beating her in order to satisfy his need for masculine self-expression. On the other hand, we have the picture of the matriarch dominating all who come within her sphere of influence, often viewed as depriving her husband of the power and influence that are rightly his. This duality is not arbitrarily conceived; it corresponds to the two aspects of family life which are fused in the middle-class image of "the family" but may well be conceptually separate for the lower class. These images, although exaggerated, do tell us something about the configuration of relationships. Marriage can turn out to be good or bad, a state of affairs that is thought to depend largely upon the qualities of the persons involved and their compatibility with each other. At certain stages of the life cycle, particularly when the woman has several small children and is highly dependent upon even inadequate support from her husband, there may be some approximation to the image of the victimized wife, forced to put up with her husband's ill-treatment for the sake of the children. However, this is a situational contingency. A woman can separate from her husband and keep a family together in various ways—by going out to work and depending upon her own mother or her older children to look after the home, by depending upon welfare, by having a boyfriend who helps out, or by a combination of these strategies. The important point is that having a husband is not an essential basis for the existence of a household. While there can be broken marriages, there is no real concept of a "broken home" in the sense used by the middle class. It may be thought desirable to have a man around the house to discipline the children, but that is very different from the idea of a basic unit forced apart.

This normative orientation does not preclude the development of close emotional ties between fathers and children. All it means is that the priority is upon ties between mothers and children, and a strain or rupture of the relationship between husband and wife affects the relationship between the father and his children much more than it does the mother–child bond. We have been struck in our investigations by the fact that relationships between fathers and children, and between ex-spouses (be they legal or nonlegal), tend to be maintained and even strengthened after the separation of the conjugal pair. A father who visits his children occasionally, gives their mother a few dollars, and takes them all out may be thought a "good" man now that he is removed from the expectations of the marital role. The contrast with the middle class is considerable. The basic standard for the middle-class male in the familial context is that he be able to support his family. The basic standard for the lower-class male turns on his masculine self-esteem, which in turn depends on his sexual and aggressive adequacy. The symbolic value of *impotence* for the lower-class man is almost equivalent to that of *incompetence* for the middle-class man. One is impressed by the frequency of the lower-class woman's complaint that her ex-husband "ran around with other women too much," and so she decided to terminate the union. Whether the husband's outside sexual activities symbolize the shift of his potency away from the marital relationship, including his financial support (which is a kind of extension of the sexual relationship), is not clear. However, it is apparent that sexual activity per se is the symbolic core of the conjugal relationship, even at the normative level; when it is transformed into other terms, it becomes support.

In discussing illegitimacy in a middle-class context, we stressed the fact that it is held to be wrong and immoral because the child has no family, its position at law is problematic, its paternity is in doubt, and its existence is an expression of the failure of its biological parents to exercise proper impulse control. The situation for the lower class is quite different. First, the position of the child in relation to the law is of minor significance, and while *some* stigma attaches to illegitimate birth, it is clearly much less important than in a middle-class setting. We do not contest the frequent assertion of welfare workers and survey specialists that lower-class women consider illegitimacy wrong and shameful. The question is, how wrong? How shameful? How abnormal? What actual consequences flow from the bearing of an illegitimate child? In what way does it affect the life chances of the mother? Most women would probably say that premarital pregnancy constituted a profound and disturbing experience, but the overall structural situation is such that premarital pregnancy did not significantly alter their life chances, which depend on quite other variables. The birth of an illegitimate child may even have resulted in improvement for some, given the present structure of welfare laws.

Attitudes toward illegitimacy differ from those of the middle class in yet another way. Rather than signifying lack of self-control, it is taken to indicate shameful disobedience, bad luck, or lack of control on the part of the parents of the girl rather than the girl herself. Most of the young mothers of illegitimate children seem to regard the pregnancy as something that "happened" to them.

Perhaps the most important difference in the position of an illegitimate child of a lower-class mother lies in the fact that its birth does not pose the same problem of structural anomaly. The lower-class pattern of kinship relations both permits and enjoins a wide-ranging network of person-to-person solidarities, and does not emphasize a restricted group of husband, wife, and their own children as the only normal domestic group. The birth of an illegitimate child to a young lower-class woman may be a great inconvenience, limiting her ability to continue school, go out to work, or "have a good time," but there is not the same feeling that this is a "fatherless child." Our data show that mothers generally go out of their way to ensure that children grow up knowing who their father is, and frequently maintain relations with the kin of their children's father or fathers. This is so whether the couple were married or never married, separated or divorced, and shows up quite clearly once one begins to collect genealogies. Illegitimate children are incorporated into viable households, whether or not those households include a man. That is, the presence of a husband/father in the household is not considered essential in quite the way it is for the middle class. This is not to say that families without a husband/father present do not experience grave difficulties, but the difficulties would not necessarily be overcome, and may be increased, by the presence of a husband/father. In short, lower-class norms facilitate the absorption of an illegitimate child with no more difficulty than if its parents were married. There may well be problems, but they do not spring solely from the marital status of the mother, since being married does not carry the same meaning of setting up an independent self-supporting domestic unit that it does for the middle-class woman.[11]

[11] Raymond T. Smith, "The Matrifocal Family," in Jack Goody (ed.), *Essays in Kinship* (Cambridge: Cambridge University Press, in press).

KINSHIP
AND THE
OCCUPATIONAL MILIEU

Chapter 5

In American culture, particularly urban American culture, the contrast between home and work can be taken to exemplify the contrast between family and the outside world, and this in turn can be understood in terms of the contrast between love and money, which stand for home and work. This contrast is much more vivid for the middle class, where the symbolic aspects of money and work are more highly elaborated, but it has meaning in lower-class cultural definitions as well. What one does at home, it is said, one does for love, not for money, while what one does at work is strictly for money. Money is material, it is power, it is impersonal and universalistic, unqualified by considerations of sentiment and morality. Relations of work and money are temporary, transient, and contingent. Love, on the other hand, is highly personal, particularistic, and beset with considerations of sentiment and morality. Whereas love is spiritual, money is material. Love is enduring and without qualification, while money is transient and contingent. Finally, in love it is personal considerations which are paramount—who the person is, not how well he performs—while with work and money, it does not matter who he is, but only how well he performs his task. Money, in this sense, is impersonal.

This neat contrast between home and work, love and money, the enduring and the transient, the universal and the particular, the moral and the material, should not blind us to the fact that, at the level of concrete action, there is a complex interplay between these two spheres of activity and domains of meaning. It takes money to maintain a home, and even though a house is not a home it is a recognized fact that a house of one's own is a good foundation for family life. A homemaker needs material to work with, and it is not unknown for people to "marry for money." Certainly it is expected that conjugal love will flow toward a *suitable* partner, and to allow considerations of love to override judgment to the point where a mistake might be made is apt to evoke disapproval for loss of self-control. It has even been known, especially among the middle class, for parents to send their children on an extended vacation so that they may "come to their senses" and "think twice" before they are "swept off their feet." This is not merely another aspect of the middle-class orientation to rationality and impulse control; the question of status is involved. American society can tolerate a fairly wide discrepancy in the status origins of married couples, and even racial differences get by these days in all except a few states, but it would be myopic to pretend that norms do not direct marital choice in directions determined at least in part by status considerations.

We could argue that these are all preliminary considerations, and that once a conjugal relationship has been entered into the norms quite clearly lay down a code for conduct which emphasizes love rather than money, the spiritual as against the material. But again, we know that this is the case only insofar as the norms are concerned. The pure kinship element in conjugal and familial roles certainly specifies a code for conduct which enjoins enduring diffuse solidarity, but other considerations which enter into the determination of actual patterns of action result in variations at the behavioral level.

The extent to which a middle-class male must make his career the basis for his family's existence has been touched upon in previous chapters, but the articulation at a behavioral level between home life and work is of a particular kind. The typical middle-class male occupation is an office job of some kind, or highly skilled work in management, commerce, or business; in short, a post in a bureaucracy. The male in such occupations can expect regular increments in pay, promotion over his career-span, and a considerable measure of security through insurance and pension schemes, including health schemes. His work almost invariably involves carefully calculated, rational procedures for decision making, accounting, designing, planning, and so on. He applies the same principles to much of the conduct of his home life (which is carefully segregated from work), and in concert with his wife and children plans every major dimension of family activities. A man who takes care of his family's welfare in this way is thought of as a good husband and father. If he gets on and does well in his job, his children and his wife can be proud of him. The extent to which his home life and his working life are segregated may vary considerably. He may have friends among his fellow employees, but, more importantly, he will probably live in a community of people who are not too different from him in age, income, and general style of life. The extent to which nuclear families of this type are "isolated" from wider kin ties has been exaggerated. When Parsons argued that the urban middle-class family tends to be isolated he clearly indicated that he meant isolated in a structural sense—in the absence of joint property holding, work, or coresidence of extended kin groups.[1] The American middle-class family is clearly not isolated from wider kin networks in the sense of having no contact with relatives, but the contacts are generally brief and social, not economic.

As we have argued in Chapter 4, norms of rationality, which are the essence of the formal structure of the bureaucratic occupational milieu, also permeate middle-class familial activities. There is doubtless a circular quality to this relationship; the child-rearing procedures of the middle class serve the occupational system, orienting young people to a career line and nurturing the proper attitudes for a methodical, carefully controlled life of successful work. Let us not get too involved in this, for there are many vexed questions about the relation between childhood experience and adult attitudes and performance; there are too many cases of lower-class children

[1] Talcott Parsons, "The Kinship System of the Contemporary United States," in *Essays in Sociological Theory* (Glencoe, Ill.: The Free Press, 1954), pp. 177–196.

becoming middle-class adults, and of middle-class children becoming confused, rebellious, or badly adjusted adults, to make us sanguine about establishing that kind of relationship with a high degree of precision. Suffice it to say that there is a certain consonance between the domestic and occupational domains.

If we turn now to the articulation between lower-class family structure and the occupational system, we are immediately faced with a problem arising from our rather crude use of the term "class." Should lower class be equated with manual workers, or blue collar workers? Should it include the unemployed, the hustlers, and the petty criminals in the same category as the affluent construction worker? Clearly such use of "class" labels conceals more than it illuminates, especially if status is the focus of attention.

There are even graver difficulties involved. Most of the literature dealing with the "problem" of lower-class family structure sees "disorganization" caused by poverty, insecurity, or disruption. We specifically reject such a simple causal relationship, particularly the notion of lower-class kinship being disorganized. The close correspondence between middle-class bureaucratic occupations and attitudes toward family life is paralleled by a similar correspondence in the lower class.

Lower-class occupations are all characterized by the fact that they do not contain the possibility of continuous promotion. They are typically either unstable, unskilled, perhaps seasonal, laboring jobs, service occupations, or skilled work with a fixed progression to the status of fully skilled worker. Some individuals may progress into supervisory or managerial positions, but that is not a normal expectation.

We have said that individualism is a characteristic American cultural orientation shared by all classes. However, it is incorporated into normative structures in differing ways; starting from the same general cultural structure, we see different transformations for each class. The lower class is just as individualistic as the rest of American society, and in some senses more so. In lower-class households there is fragmentation of finances, with each individual feeling both a right to his or her own resources and an obligation to give to others in need. It is a highly individualized network of reciprocal person-to-person ties. There is no concept of a long-term "budget" for a "family." In a city the sheer need to meet regular payments for rent, utilities, and so on, imposes some centrality on finances. Welfare payments are often accompanied by gratuitous advice on how the money could or should be spent. None of this creates a spirit of long-term centralized budget planning. The dominant pattern is one of frequent small flows of cash and goods along widely spreading kinship links. Families with more stable and adequate sources of income may approximate middle-class patterns, with a heavy investment in schooling for children directed toward mobility. This merely indicates that class does not manifest itself in groups with sharply drawn boundaries.

Lower-class persons certainly show a strong desire to improve the physical condition of their lives, but this should not lead us to think of them as thwarted or deprived but essentially middle-class Americans. It is more important to distinguish between sheer income level and class identity as it applies to the lower class than it is with other classes. There are many poor people in America who are neither lower class nor working class. To equate the poor with the lower class gives rise to such old middle-class notions as the "culture of poverty." The cultural orientation of the lower class can be found among people who are quite well off, just as there are many genteel poor of undoubted middle-class orientation.

The norms of individualism among the lower class are expressed in the conception of the individual's right to respect, as well as in the freedom to align and realign himself in varying patterns of solidarity with others. Whereas the middle-class person is responsive to signals of approval for his performance, the lower-class person is typically sensitive to any suggestions that he is not intrinsically worthy. If the middle-class person perceives signs of disapproval, he will be embarrassed and resolve to try to do better next time. The lower-class person is indifferent to disapproval of performance, but will react violently to any suggestion that he is "less than a man"; that is, to an attack upon his attributes as a person.

Norms governing attitudes toward work among the lower class

differ considerably from middle-class standards, being quite negative by comparison. Lower-class workers look forward to increased wages, but not through promotion up a career line. Pay increases through collective bargaining or individual overtime are the normal methods of increasing purchasing power, or, in these days of inflation, simply maintaining purchasing power.

Another aspect of lower-class normative patterns for individualism is seen in expenditure patterns. Whereas middle-class spending is concentrated in family purchases which enhance or maintain the status and prestige of the whole family through maintenance of the family home, vacations, cultural activities, and so on, lower-class expenditures tend to be highly individualized and directed toward maintaining the appearance and prestige of individuals. Of course, the basic expenditures on such necessities as rent, food, and utility bills consume a much larger proportion of lower-class income, and there is often nothing left over for personal spending. When there is, the spending is frequently generous, and by middle-class standards extravagant and foolish.

The congruence of work norms and experience and family normative structure is not fortuitous, of course. Work is an important expression of sex-role differentiation, and both occupational status and sex-role are intrinsic dimensions of the conglomerate familial roles at the level of the normative system. In this sense, occupational roles interpenetrate familial roles and help to constitute them.

SEX-ROLE COMPONENTS IN KINSHIP AND FAMILY NORMS

Chapter **6**

We have outlined the ways in which the norms of family life and kinship vary between middle and lower class. We have also suggested that the normative system contains elements which derive from a variety of different cultural domains, and that each such domain contributes a "pure" cultural element to the normative system. The normative system is thus a conglomerate from the point of view of its cultural content, for it contains elements from a variety of different pure cultural domains. At the normative level, the level which specifies how roles should be played, the kinship component from the pure domain of kinship is joined to components from various other pure cultural domains such as sex, age, and a variety of others. Thus a father at the normative level (and the status of father does not exist except at the normative level) contains components from the kinship domain, the age domain, the sex domain, and other pure cultural domains as well.

We have suggested that there are significant differences in the norms of family life and kinship relations between middle class and the lower class, and the question before us now is how to account for those differences.

We have said that the kinship component in these norms does not vary from class to class in America, using the term "kinship component" in the technical sense of its "pure cultural" form as we have defined it above. Thus we have demonstrated that the fundamental definition of a relative is always the same, regardless of class. He is a person related by blood or by marriage; sexual union is the distinctive feature of kinship; and relatives are distinguished from nonrelatives by their special relationship of enduring, diffuse solidarity. The "pure cultural" elements are incorporated into the norms of both middle and lower class without change or transformation, and they are the same in the norms of both classes.

If the differences in the normative system of kinship and family between middle and lower class cannot be accounted for or traced to differences in the kinship component, how can those differences be explained?

It is our contention that the variations between middle- and lower-class kinship and family norms (set out briefly in Chapter 4) are due primarily to variations in the sex-role component of the norms.

We therefore turn now to a fuller discussion of sex-role, dealing first with the most general cultural definitions and meanings of "sex."

Initially, this problem can be approached in just the same way as the problem of kinship: by first asking what are the distinctive or defining features of sex as these are defined in American culture.

Cultural Definitions
of Sex and Sex-Roles

"Sex," in its cultural definition, consists in two major parts. One has to do with coitus, sexual intercourse, erotic activity. The other has to do with maleness and femaleness. The former is the *marked* value, the latter *unmarked*.[1] It is marked in that, in its narrowest sense, "sex" means coitus. But in a wider, more inclusive sense, "sex" means much more than that; it means *all* of the different

[1] Joseph Greenberg, *Language Universals* (The Hague: Mouton & Co., 1966).

parts of maleness and femaleness that do not directly enter into coitus or erotic activity, yet are considered to be within the domain of sex, along with the marked feature, coitus itself. The unmarked meaning is thus wider and encompasses the marked, narrower, and more highly specific meaning.

The two major parts of the cultural definition of sex, then can be called, first the domain of sexual *intercourse* and second the domain of sexual *attributes*.

In American culture, a person is defined as male or female by the kind of sexual organs he has. Although a child is not a man or a woman until sexually mature, its identity as male or female is established at birth by the kind of genitals it has.[2] There are, in addition, certain characteristics which are indicators of sex identity. Men have facial hair and are said to have hair on their chests, but women do not. Temperamental differences are believed to correlate with the differences in sexual organs. Men are said to have an active, women a passive, quality. Men have greater physical strength and stamina than women. Men are said to have mechanical aptitudes that women lack. Women have warm, nurturant qualities which men lack. Men tend toward an aggressive disposition said to be absent in women. These commonly held beliefs are examples of what might be called *concomitant features* of sexual identity, and whether there is any actual scientific basis for these beliefs is not at issue here.

The difference between a culturally *distinctive or defining* feature and *concomitant* features is quite clear if we review some simple examples. Men have facial hair, women do not. From the fact that the bearded lady at the circus is counted as a lady, it follows that facial hair is not the defining feature. Men are active and aggressive, women passive. From the fact that an aggressive woman can be criticized for being "too masculine" but remain an aggres-

---

[2] This determination is not often difficult to make, but it may be in certain cases. For some problems in this area, as well as for a brilliant study of the distinctive features of this domain of sex, see H. Garfinkel, *Studies in Ethnomethodology* (Englewood Cliffs, N.J.: Prentice-Hall, Inc., 1967), pp. 116–185, 285–288.

sive woman, it follows that activity is not the distinctive feature of sex. If a person dresses in female clothing, lacks facial hair, has long head-hair, is passive, but has male genitalia, that person is classed as a male. Genitals, then, are the distinctive feature in terms of which male and female are defined in American culture.

There is an obvious and striking parallel between the way in which the whole domain of sex is defined and the way in which kinship is defined in American culture. The domain of sex is divided into the subdomains of intercourse and attributes, while the domain of kinship is derived from the major domains of law and nature. In each case the division is between an *attribute*, or set of apparently concrete properties, and an *interactive or relational* part. Thus the domain of nature is conceived of as having certain concrete properties of objects which "are," while the domain of law has relational or interactional qualities; the domain of sexual attributes like the domain of nature has properties of objects which "are," while the domain of sexual intercourse is relational or interactional just as is the domain of law. These two oppositions, appear to be derived one from the other, that is, each is a direct derivative of the master opposition between the *order of nature* and the *order of law*, the former having *attributive* qualities, the latter *interactional* (or *relational*) qualities. The opposition between the order of nature and the order of law has a fundamental place in the organization of American culture.

Put in these terms, the parallel suggests that a single symbol that is culturally defined as sex is the model in terms of which both the sex-role and the kinship domains are defined and differentiated. The sex-role system takes that aspect of the cultural definition of sex having to do with sexual attributes as its model or symbol. The kinship system rests on the cultural definition of sexual intercourse as its model or symbol. Differentiation within each subsystem proceeds according to the same opposition between attributes and interaction (or relationship), one in terms of the nature/law opposition, the other in terms of the opposition of sexual attributes and a relational element to be specified below. Finally, the relationship between the sex-role or attributes system and the sexual intercourse or kinship system is that of unmarked to marked categories, or encompassing to encompassed,[3] in that the latter is included as a distinct part of the former.

If the opposition at the most general level is one of attribute versus interaction or relation, then the second value in the opposition specific to the sex-role or sex attributes system should be a special kind of relationship or interaction, just as "law" is a special kind of interaction or relationship in the kinship system. What is that special kind of interaction?

Sexual intercourse, as the symbol in terms of which kinship is defined and differentiated, is a symbol for unity—physical, spiritual, emotional—for the coming together into a single whole, for the bringing of opposites together, for the inseparability and interdependence of the differentiated parts, for enduring or "eternal" solidarity, and so on.[4] Note that it is the unity of separate and different things which is the stressed element in the combination of components here. It is the bringing together of two people, each of opposite sex, the holding together of father, mother, and child in one whole, called the family, that is emphasized. It is the creation of unity out of difference.

In the case of sexual attributes, the same components are put in the opposite relationship to each other in regard to the emphasis of their symbolic meaning. Here the symbol stresses separating rather than unifying, differentiating rather than bringing together. Here similarities are subordinated to differences and the unity of the whole domain of sex is left implicit, while its divergent, differentiating, oppositional quality is emphasized.

It is in this sense that the unspecified part of the equation noted above is interactional or relational. The two sexes are, and take their meaning from, their differences, their divergence, their oppositional qualities. Each is oriented toward the other as contrary, opposite, different from. It is this burden of emphasizing

[3] See Louis Dumont, *Homo Hierarchicus* (Chicago: University of Chicago Press, 1970), pp. xii, 231–238, for a discussion of the logical structure of such a relationship.

[4] See David M. Schneider, *American Kinship: A Cultural Account* (Englewood Cliffs, N.J.: Prentice-Hall, Inc., 1968).

difference from the other, that, at the level of the individual actor, creates the stress of identity crises which Freud and Erikson have described. It is this burden of emphasizing the difference from the other that makes the diacritical marks of sex, the concomitant features like hair and activity or passivity, so heavily laden with deeply emotional significance.

Put in somewhat different terms, the special quality of interaction or relation where sex-role is concerned is the emphasis on the distinctive and differentiated quality of each sex, on the marks of difference and the nature of the differences, each with reference to the other. The stress or emphasis is explicitly on difference and apartness, and it is interactional or relational in this special sense of a system of diacritical marks for the definition and maintenance of difference with respect to each other.

It is obvious that the differences between the sexes are defined as complementary, that they are differences with respect to single dimensions, that the differences are such as to create an interdependence between them so that one is meaningless without the other. It is precisely this which characterizes Durkheim's notion of organic solidarity; differentiated marks of identity define units so that no unit can be self-sufficient in either of two different ways —in its cultural definition or in its social functions—but each must depend on the other unit for its definition as well as for the completion of some task or array of tasks. Insofar as sex-role is concerned, the emphasis or the stress of the definitional elements is on difference and apartness, not on interdependence and unity. These latter meanings exist in the definitions, but they are subordinated to, and encompassed by, the stress on difference and apartness. However much there may be a unit at a functional level, however much there may be an actually recognized interdependence, these aspects are nevertheless subordinated to the meanings of apartness and distinctiveness at the level of cultural meaning and symbols.

In summary, we have said that there are two sexes and have given the cultural definition of those two sexes. The cultural definition rests specifically on the difference between the form of the genitalia, but concomitant features are assigned each sex in addition to the culturally defining features. According to their cultural dimensions, the two sexes are in two different kinds of relationship. On the one hand, the relationship of sexual intercourse or coitus has the cultural meaning of unifying differences and producing a unit out of that interaction. On the other hand, the attributive meaning of sex is such that the emphasis is on maintaining differences despite the implicit or inherent interdependence between the two differently defined elements of male and female. In the former the cultural stress is on unity; in the latter the cultural stress is on diversity. In the former the implicit subordinated element is that diverse elements exist which can be unified. In the latter the implicit, subordinated element is that, however much of a whole, unified thing the two sexes may be—in intercourse or in any other form of functional interdependence—it is nevertheless their distinctiveness and difference which is stressed. In the former the "problem" is to bring the different units together to become one. In the latter the "problem" is to establish and to maintain, despite countervailing tendencies, the differences and distinctiveness of each unit. In the former the value of difference is subordinated to, and encompassed by, unity. In the latter the value of difference is stressed, superordinate to, and encompasses the subordinate unity.

There is, finally, the inequality of the sexes which is a significant feature of the whole system. Equality/inequality are quite distinct from the nature of the sexes and their differences, so that the sexes might be defined as different but equal, or different but unequal. The definition of the situation of men and women in American culture is that they are different and unequal, men being held superior to women. Yet the inequality of the sexes has a different value in the two major domains of sex. In the domain of intercourse, which is the domain of kinship, it is the unification of the sexes that is stressed in the symbol of coitus, and this message of unity, harmony, and identity overrides the value of inequality, although the inequality remains clearly present. It is as if the value of unity, which seems to imply equality but does not really, is stressed, while the premise of inequality is left in a residual position.

On the other hand, the sex attribute or sex-role system stresses the differences between the sexes and does so in such a way as to give equal stress to their inequality as well, so that under some phrasings it is almost impossible to sort out elements which are simply different from those which are also unequal.

There is an interesting historical note to be added here. During the nineteenth century it was common to assert a pronounced difference between European and American family life. Alexis de Tocqueville, for example, was impressed by the extent to which the progress of democracy had already affected family life. He remarked upon the pervasive sense of equality between men and women:

> An American girl scarcely ever displays that virginal softness in the midst of young desires or that innocent and ingenuous grace which usually attend the European woman in the transition from girlhood to youth. It is rare that an American woman at any age displays childish timidity or ignorance.[5]

He noted, however, that the disappearance of a sense of inequality between men and women did not lead to an erasure of the distinction of function; on the contrary, American women were more firmly devoted to hearth, home, and the raising of children than their European counterparts.

Another European observer, Harriett Martineau, reached different conclusions from the same kind of observation. She complained that while the wealth and open nature of American society afforded the greatest opportunity for the reduction of inequality between the sexes, the American women are, if anything, less well represented in traditionally male occupations than they are in Europe.[6]

Both these observers are correct, but they are talking about different things. Tocqueville is referring to the interactional aspect

[5] Alexis de Tocqueville, *Democracy in America* (New York: Vintage Books, 1957), Vol. II, p. 209.
[6] Harriett Martineau, *Society in America* (New York: Doubleday & Company, Inc., 1962).

of sex-role definition and is right in his contention that men and women demonstrate a considerable sense of equality, companionship, and cooperation in the familial domain, a fact reflected in women's generally more confident and self-assured demeanor. In the occupational milieu the attributes of the sexes are stressed as the basis for allocation to different tasks, and here women continue to be markedly "unequal," as Harriett Martineau observed.

The whole domain of sex, intercourse and attributes, is defined as being biological, as rooted, grounded, fixed by, or determined by the biological nature of mankind. It is then but a special part of the larger domain of nature, and is distinguished from other domains of nature by the fact that it is defined in terms of genitalia. The domain of sex, like other domains within nature, is defined as "given," "inherent," "biological," or "biologically determined." Sexual impulses are defined as "instinctive." The behavior of a woman toward her child is also defined as being governed by instincts, and the fierce, often irrational, way in which mothers are believed to protect their children is defined as being quite natural, something given by nature and not easily learned or taught or subject to cultural constraint.[7]

These definitions apply throughout the different parts of American society and American culture. They are not confined to or distinctive of any particular segment of it. Both lower and middle class define masculinity and femininity in the same general terms. The differences lie in the manner in which these qualities are embodied in social roles, and of course the roles themselves vary according to where the relevant persons stand in terms of the occupational and status systems, and they vary according to the more general orientations which are characteristic of the different classes.

---

[7] It goes without saying that whether any of these statements have any scientific validity as facts of biology has no direct bearing on the problem before us. In American culture, beliefs about biology serve as a theory of both kinship and sex-role differentiation. It is this cultural theory that is the issue here. Whether the cultural theory also corresponds with any or all of the known biological facts is not a problem, for we are not investigating what determines cultural constructs or what determines changes in them. We are only asking, "What *are* the cultural constructs?" For a more extended discussion of this problem and the problem of cultural symbolism, see the conclusion to Schneider, *American Kinship*, pp. 107–117.

Sex-Roles and Social Action

We turn now to a more detailed examination of the normative patterns of male and female activity; this requires some understanding of the interrelationship of the cultural component of social roles and the exigencies of social system organization, though we are obliged to compress our discussion into model structures or "ideal types."

Lower-class women generally experience sexual intercourse and child-bearing at an earlier age than middle-class women; frequently their introduction to sexual relations is both abrupt and violent, or so it seems to them in retrospect, though this may be nothing more than a statement to the effect that it was not planned. Take for example the case of Mrs. Eddy, 43 years old, daughter of an immigrant Norwegian carpenter and odd-job man who married a waitress. When Mrs. Eddy was asked how she met her husband, she said: "I met him in an institution; I was 16. I had been put away for being raped." The rape had occurred late at night after a movie show which she had attended with her brother. Although she left with her brother, he ran ahead. "I had to pass a back alley so this guy jumped out and he grabbed me and he pulled me into an alley and threw me into a gangway. I had just started my period. He threw me into a basement and tore all my clothes off. . . . My mother took me to the doctor and I was torn in four places inside my body and the doctor said 'Well, her period's liable to stop on her.' " Sure enough, she turned out to be pregnant.

Of course, this woman's story of her induction into sexual experience is far from being a simple factual account. She condenses into odd juxtaposed shapes a whole mass of experience, meaning, fantasy, and fear. However, the central message is clear: sex and her relationship with the father of her first child were abrupt, unplanned, and violent. In fact, it must lead us to ask whether intercourse was involved at all, except in a very narrow and technical sense. She claims that she did not even see the boy, though somehow he was later identified by a girlfriend. These early sexual encounters are frequently of this nature; over and over again the word "rape" crops up, with all its connotations of aggressive, violent, negative intercourse. The lower-class girl who actually enjoys the company of boys is generally characterized as an "easy lay," and has a multitude of liaisons confined almost solely to sexual intercourse in the limited sense of quick coitus.

We should ask ourselves whether this pattern of relations between boys and girls is actually evidence of early stress upon sexual *intercourse* or sexual *attributes* in the sense we outlined above. If one contrasts this with the middle-class pattern, certain interesting facts emerge. By the age of 12 middle-class children are apt to form cross-sex friendships, even though some latent hostility persists. The normative emphasis is upon friendly cooperation in class and in social events. There is differentiation and the stressing of attributes, of course; girls play some different games, take some different school subjects, wear different clothes, and have some different interests. But the stress is upon a convergence of interests. Girls are increasingly oriented toward a college education and take virtually the same academic subjects as boys. The friendships between teen-age boys and girls involve them in common activities expressing common tastes in music, poetry, films, plays, politics, books, and party-going.

The lower class *pattern* is just the opposite. (We stress *pattern* here because it is clear that one cannot make a simple separation of empirical cases to fit these models.) Boys and girls diverge as they approach their teens and the stress continues to be upon this separation, with social intercourse taking a subsidiary, though increasingly important, part. The orientation of lower-class teen-agers is toward life chances, academic training, and occupational opportunities which are quite different from the middle class, and also vary between lower-class boys and girls. The social relations of lower-class teen-agers are overwhelmingly with groups of the same sex, and although a particular boy and a particular girl may be linked, this does not mean that they spend time alone together or develop a close friendship based on common interests. They meet as members of groups, and the whole pattern of relationship appears hostile, differentiated, teasing, bantering, and full of apparent aggression. The stress is upon sexual *attributes* and not sexual *intercourse* in its wider, interactional, sense.

These variations by social class are seen in formal school work as well as in informal peer group activities. Approximately 46.5 percent of all high school pupils in the U.S. now go to college; 75.4 percent now finish high school and the rest drop out at some stage.[8] There is a high correlation between college entry and father's occupation, but perhaps even more important is the high correlation between *intention* to go to college, ability as measured by intelligence tests, and father's occupation. It is the intention factor which is important in sorting students into different kinds of high school courses, and ultimately into different occupations. Children from the lowest status families not only attend overcrowded schools with the lowest percentage of qualified teachers, but they are much more oriented toward going into lower status occupations—or rebelling against the system altogether. However, leaving aside the issue of disparities in the quality of public education for different classes in America, the interesting point is that lower-class youth tend toward more marked sex-role differentiation in all activities during adolescence. In classes there is more separation into such "vocationally oriented" courses as shopwork, engineering drawing, and applied mathematics for boys and shorthand, typing, cooking, or domestic science for girls. In peer group activities participation in sports is an immediate means of segregation by sex, and the widespread existence of youth gangs in lower-class schools is also indicative of the separation. The development of female gangs, sometimes linked in a tenuous way to the male gangs, merely reinforces the sex-role differentiation.[9]

The middle-class school still displays considerable continuing sex-role differentiation, but the tendency is for it to be minimized

---

[8] U.S. Bureau of the Census, *Statistical Abstract of the United States: 1971* (92d. edition), Washington, D.C., 1971, pp. 109, 125.

[9] See R. Lincoln Keiser, *The Vice Lords: Warriors of the Streets* (New York: Holt, Rinehart & Winston, 1969), for an excellent account of a Chicago gang.

in both formal work and peer group activities. Girls have as much, or nearly as much, expectation of going to college, even though the consciousness of an ultimate role as mother and wife is ever present. The pressure upon girls to compete equally with boys in the academic and occupational spheres has been growing steadily over the past 20 years. This does not mean that sex differences are ignored or become unimportant. On the contrary, they are a considerable pre-occupation, but the stress is upon social conformity to an ideal of loving interaction and companionship, rather than upon the different attributes of males and females.[10] It is understood that boys and girls who are going together will engage in activities involving similar interests. Doubtless one of those interests is physical contact, which is not only permissible but enjoined. However, its aim is not sexual intercourse for its own sake, and the whole relationship should reflect the couple's regard for each other and their controlled response to the situation. Dramatic changes in sexual behavior among young people seem to have occurred over the last decade, with full sexual intercourse being experienced at increasingly lower ages. The evidence is difficult to interpret but it seems that while the overall rate of teen-age sexual intercourse is increasing, there is maintenance of the class differential with poorer girls experiencing sexual intercourse at an earlier age and in greater numbers.[11] It seems likely that increased knowledge and use of birth control techniques will extend petting and necking to full genital intercourse, but the same pattern of control, stress on personal interaction, and "love" will prevail, as against the momentary joining of distinct sexual attributes.

If this argument is approximately correct (it should be remembered that we are trying to analyze elements which enter into

[10] This differs not only from the lower-class, but also from the upper-class pattern, where there is much more emphasis upon female beauty, dress, taste, and general cultural expertise, while men are more likely to prepare themselves for leadership roles, and in their leisure time stress such symbolic masculine activities as hunting, sailing, or flying. We shall discuss the intermediate pattern of the "working class" more fully below.

[11] See John F. Kanter and Melvin Zelnik, "Sexual Experience of Young Unmarried Women in the United States," in *Family Planning Perspectives*, Vol. 4, No. 4, October 1972, pp. 9–18.

role structure, not describe behavior), then what are attributes, and how and why are they differentially structured by class? Ultimately the distinctive attributes of sex are male and female genitalia, but the concomitant features are more elaborated, capable of more complex cultural definition, and more tightly enmeshed in social system structure and social action.[12] These concomitant features include not only such physical features as breasts, facial hair, voice timbre, or such supposed "natural" characteristics as strength and aggression versus delicacy and passivity, but also run the whole gamut of differentiated patterns of social activity.

Perhaps the most fundamental aspect of the differentiation of activity by sex is in the realm of work. We know that such a differentiation exists in all societies, and that it cannot be explained in terms of the simple facts of difference of biological function. Exaggerated though they may be, the contrasts which Margaret Mead draws[13] do point up the extent to which it is possible to liberate sex-roles from sex physiology. Levi-Strauss, following Durkheim's view of organic solidarity, has argued that the purpose of differentiation of social roles by sex is to increase the dependence of males and females upon each other, and thus further their solidarity. No doubt this is so at certain levels of social and economic differentiation, but it is not immediately apparent that sex-role differentiation is necessary in a complex and functionally differentiated social system. On the contrary, it seems more likely that the persistence of marked sex-role differentiation in the occupational sphere is linked to a conception of certain kinds of activity being inappropriate to women, and others being inappropriate to men, even though such differentiation is unnecessary as a means of producing solidarity at any macrosocietal level.

There is a marked distinction in American culture between

[12] It is interesting that as sex-role differentiation decreases in the modern middle class, there is a diminution in the significance of secondary or concomitant features, and the focus upon the genitalia becomes more pronounced. The pictorial, literary, and dramatic focus upon penis and vagina is quite remarkable in this sense. Conversely, the lower class tends to regard nudity as being "dirty," and emphasizes the secondary sexual characteristics and concomitant features much more.

[13] Margaret Mead, *Sex and Temperament in Three Primitive Societies* (New York: William Morrow & Co., 1935).

the occupational domain, dominated by men, and the domestic domain, which is considered to be a more appropriately female area of action. The sharp and unequivocal separation of work and home is not intrinsically linked to sex-role differentiation, but is an aspect of what Weber called "bureaucratization"—that is, the transcendence of a purely kinship-based system of production and a patrimonial system of authority.[14] Continuing differentiation by sex in the occupational sphere (in any sphere, for that matter) is contrary to the spirit of rationalization and bureaucratization, which sets the value of objective standards of performance and the rational enactment and observance of rules above all else.

Before that ideal state is reached, there is much room for the interference of a subsidiary emphasis upon such particularistic qualities as sex or race, and whatever the historical trend toward increasing rationality, we know that an emphasis upon efficiency can be shaped into an ideology for furthering the interests of a particular class.

It seems likely, for example, that modern complex society will continue to require a large body of relatively unskilled and service workers. Perhaps more accurately, there will continue to be such a lag in the demand for highly skilled personnel that it will not be crucial to ensure that all children are highly trained.[15] It is probable that the educational system will continue to service the economy in the way it has in the past, and the middle and upper classes will continue to ensure that their children are properly trained for high income positions. It is also more likely that the female children of the middle class will increasingly meet the demand for highly skilled personnel, thereby making it more difficult to justify in economic terms the wholesale upgrading of lower-class education. It is difficult to see middle-class women foregoing marriage and family, so if they do enter the labor force in large numbers there

---

[14] Max Weber, *The Theory of Social and Economic Organization* (Glencoe, Ill.: The Free Press, 1947), pp. 324–340.

[15] Recent studies show an increase in the proportion of the labor force engaged in white collar activities to over 50 percent, with a corresponding decline in agricultural and blue collar employment. The proportion of workers in service industries is increasing.

will be an increased demand for labor in the service industries. Any large-scale and significant shift away from the present domination of values stressing work, achievement, consumption, and individual enterprise seems unlikely, in spite of the prevalence of middle-class youth radicalism and the demand for a more humane use of economic resources.

It is against this background that one must see the continuing distinction between classes in the United States, and the variations in sex-role differentiation. It is unlikely that service occupations will be radically reorganized and upgraded in status, so we may expect a continuation of the pattern of instability and marked sex-linked differentiation there. Even though these service occupations are unattractive to many employees, they will continue to be the only source of income for large numbers of people, short of a massive reorganization of the whole economic and social system.

The working class clearly represents an intermediate stage between the ideal-type cases of the lower and middle classes. Although the working class is oriented toward mobility of a certain kind, it is mobility toward a state of greater security. Buying a home, building a savings account, and having enough left over to satisfy a deep craving for the consumption of material goods is the characteristic orientation of this segment of the population. This is basically a lower-class orientation, despite the apparent similarity to middle-class status mobility striving. It certainly contains within itself the whole range of lower-class cultural orientations toward sex-role differentiation and their expression in occupational and other activities.

There is some evidence that working-class women are more "middle class" than the men in their cultural orientation. They are frequently disappointed in their husband's failure to provide emotional support and response;[16] they often show more desire to push the children beyond high school; they are less convinced of the value

[16] See Lee Rainwater, Richard P. Coleman, and Gerald Handel, *Workingman's Wife* (New York: Oceana Publications, Inc., 1959). It would be interesting to measure the relationship between the wife's dissatisfaction with a high level of segregation of conjugal roles, and the intensity of her participation in external networks, particularly networks of kin ties.

of authoritarian procedures in child-rearing. For the working-class girl, being a wife is as important an aspect of mature womanhood as being a mother, and she is likely to think of her future role as a mother within the context of a stable home life based upon marriage.

The major component of being working class, as opposed to lower class, is the greater security and higher earnings of males, which makes for a firmer economic base for conjugal unions. However, it does not create a middle-class pattern of normative expectations. A marked stress upon sex-role differentiation persists, along with considerable segregation of conjugal roles and a continuing proliferation of ties linking members of the immediate family to other kin. Even where such external relations are attenuated, or severed, as in the case of the automobile plant workers in California described by Bennett Berger, the pattern created is not middle class, but merely a disfigured and impoverished version of lower-class kinship norms.[17]

[17] Bennett Berger, *Working-class Suburb: A Study of Auto Workers in Suburbia* (Berkeley: University of California Press, 1960).

THE FAMILY, HOUSEHOLD COMPOSITION, AND CHILD-REARING

Chapter 7

Almost any general work dealing with the family is likely to contain a simple story of human history which goes something like this. Because of the manner in which human beings reproduce, and because the human infant needs prolonged care in order to survive physically and develop culturally, there has always been some kind of enduring group structure to perform the tasks of child-nurturance and rearing. Since women bear and feed infants, are attached to them by instinct, and are generally weaker than males, a division of labor by sex has developed quite naturally, and this makes men and women dependent upon each other in a general social sense. Given the further fact that culture is distinctively human and consists in a body of transmissible knowledge and rules for behavior which have to be emotionally as well as cognitively absorbed, children have to be socialized in small groups, and these groups are most conveniently termed "the family."

Such speculations about the nature of human history are very old. In a book published in 1881, E. B. Tylor wrote:

> . . . the ruder kinds of family union among savages and bar-
> barians shows that there cannot be expected from them the
> excellence of those well-ordered households to which civilised
> society owes so much of its goodness and prosperity. Yet even
> among the rudest clans of men, unless depraved by vice or

misery and falling to pieces, a standard of family morals is known and lived by. Their habits, judged by our notions, are hard and coarse, yet the family tie of sympathy and common interest is already formed, and the foundations of moral duty already laid, in the mother's patient tenderness, the father's desperate valour in defence of home, their daily care for the little ones, the affection of brothers and sisters and the mutual forbearance, helpfulness and trust of all.[1]

One cannot imagine that being written in quite the same way today, but many elements of more sophisticated latter-day views of the family are clearly stated there, and of course the general structure of these ideas can be traced much further back in European history. The central functional idea is that of the family as a coresidential, cooperating group consisting of a father and a mother jointly engaged in child-rearing.

As we pointed out at the beginning of this monograph, generations of anthropological research have informed us that many societies seem to have developed other ways of organizing their domestic institutions, and consequently quite sophisticated methods have been devised for the analysis of household composition in different societies. From very simple typologies expressed in terms of whether "marriage" was "matrilocal" or "patrilocal" we have progressed through distinctions in terms of "virilocality" and "uxorilocality" and "neolocality" to consideration of developmental cycles whereby static survey data are converted into more dynamic models of the manner in which kinship relations are entered into, develop over time, and decay. There are still sharp limits to the validity of these procedures, and in this work we intend merely to draw attention to alternative ways of approaching the study of kinship relations and their incorporation in varying forms of domestic unit.

American sociology has long been concerned with problems of family disorganization, to the extent that we would regard this concern as a peculiarly national preoccupation were it not that the European literature of the nineteenth and early twentieth centuries

[1] Edward Burnett Tylor, *Anthropology, An Introduction to the Study of Man and Civilisation* (New York: D. Appleton & Co., 1916), p. 405.

also concentrates on the same problems. The most recent outpouring of concern has focused on the "Negro family," and therefore we begin our discussion with the presentation of a case from our interview records. While this is by no means an average case, it has many features which are typical in a more profound sense, as may be judged by comparing it with an increasing number of published reports of similarly collected case histories. What is particularly striking is the contrast between material collected in this way and the more usual sociological data derived from surveys or short interviews around particular topics.[2] On the question of whether it is possible to generalize from lower-class Black family structure to the lower class generally, we make no final judgment at this stage. What is clear is that the major variables affecting domestic organization are present in the lower class generally; if it turns out that domestic organization differs significantly between lower-class Black and lower-class White, we would be inclined to seek the source of the differences in the manner in which the same variables operate differentially between the groups, rather than in some specifically "racial" variable. This is an issue we take up again later.

Patricia Walker is 40 years old, rather heavy, the mother of seven children ranging in age from 4 to 22 years. She lives in Woodlawn, a virtually all-Black area on Chicago's South Side, having moved there from the Robert Taylor Homes, a city housing project, about the horrors of which she can wax quite eloquent. Born in Louisiana in 1930, she was her mother's only child, born when her mother was 13 and her father 14. They were married but separated after only one year, when her father headed for another town. He ended up in Chicago, where he lives with his common-law wife and Patricia's half-siblings. Patricia was brought up by her mother, who worked as a domestic servant and nursemaid for a well-off White family; she (the mother) has worked with the same family in the South for the past 23 years and has raised their three children.

---

[2] See, for example, Carol B. Stack, "The Kindred of Viola Jackson: Residence and Family Organization of an Urban Black American Family," in Whitten and Szwed, eds., *Afro-American Anthropology* (New York: The Free Press, 1970), pp. 303–311. Compare this account with the picture one gets from reading L. Rainwater, *Behind Ghetto Walls* (Chicago: Aldine Publishing Co., 1970).

She did not marry again and has never had any more children of her own. Patricia says she was spoiled as a child; her mother bought her lots of clothes and always saw that she was well turned out for school, even though she had to go without herself. While she was growing up she and her mother lived in a three-room house with her mother's mother. Her grandmother's husband had died after having fathered 14 children, of which only 4 survived. The grandmother married again but had no other children, and Patricia's memory of this stepgrandfather is of a somewhat stupid man who drank a lot and was constantly being ridiculed by her grandmother.

Patricia would go out a lot as a girl to dances with friends, even in other towns, and she made a great deal of the fact that her mother really trusted her and let her stay out late.

When she was 19 she became pregnant. The father was James Williams, a married man who lived close by. He now lives in Chicago, somewhere on the West Side, but she has not seen him for about six years. The baby was born in March and in July she got married—not to James Williams, but to Lawrence Tyler, a boy she had known for a long time in school. She says, "We met each other in school. We grew up together more or less. I guess I married him because of Charles (her son) but I was crazy; otherwise I wouldn't have married nobody at my age. I had a wonderful childhood; at least I have that because he turned out no good." Still, he fathered her next two children and they still see quite a lot of him in Chicago, where he now lives with another woman. (They have no children, though she had four from a previous union.) Patricia Walker moved to Chicago in 1953. By that time she had left Lawrence Tyler and gone back to live with her mother. The reason she decided to move to Chicago was that so many other people from her hometown were coming up here, including many of her relatives. In her own words: "They comes down south in their shiny big cars and their nice clothes and tells us that they're making 50 or 60 dollars a week. They don't tell us that they bought the clothes and cars on credit and that the rent and food eats up most of that 50 or 60. When I lived in Bellville [in Louisiana] we lived in a three-room house for $3.50 a week. But we was all anxious to get up north and make some of it too. I was the same way. And I decided I was going to get me some of it too. They didn't say it was nothing but work, work, work, and that's what it's been. Ever since I've been old enough, all I've done is work—and I mean *hard* work."

That certainly seems to be true. She worked first as a domestic servant, but found the female employers too demanding of "respect"; they expected her to address their children as "Miss" or "Master" and to engage in various other demeaning acts of submission, so she gave that up. She got a job in the kitchen of a hospital which was better paid, but also much harder work. Next she worked as a cleaner for the Chicago Transit Authority, cleaning buses and trains. That was the hardest job of all but the pay was much better than anything else she has had. When the work got too hard she found a job as a waitress in a snack bar, and from there became a cashier in a small 5 & 10¢ store, a job she lost when the store was burned down in the Martin Luther King riots. The snack bar was glad to take her back as a waitress, and that is where she is now.

While doing all this she managed to bring up her seven children apparently single-handedly. After she got to Chicago she had two children as a result of friendships with men with whom she was friendly but never considered marrying. She is still on good terms with the fathers of these two children, who drop in occasionally and give the children things. One has become a dope addict and was in jail for selling heroin. In 1958 she married Raymond Walker, her present husband (it seems unlikely that she was ever actually divorced from her first husband, but this does not weigh heavily on her mind). Raymond Walker has had a series of jobs of various kinds, all of which require little skill and are very insecure. When he can he works as a laborer on building sites, but he has also worked in car washes, as a cleaner in a factory, and with a small contractor engaged in painting, decorating, and wall washing. Her two youngest children were fathered by Raymond Walker, from whom she is now separated. He is living up on the North Side of Chicago with his mother. "We have been separated since September 1968. We have what you'd call a friendly separation. I just couldn't take him running around. But we're real friendly; he calls me almost every day and brings me money on his payday. Like yesterday, he calls me here and asks me if me and the kids need a ride home from the restaurant. I said yeah and he picked me and the kids up and took us home. When I was getting out of the car he asked me if I needed any money and he gave me $20.00.

"Lulu Belle, Raymond's mother, and I are good friends. I see her about once a week and talk to her a lot on the phone. She lives on the North Side. My kids are going up there this week to stay with her for five days—the younger kids that is, except Junior. He's afraid to leave me; he thinks she's going to keep him, as if anybody would want to keep him 'cept me."

She is very proud of the fact that she has a granddaughter, Janice Williams. Janice is her eldest son's daughter. "The baby lives with his mother and grandmother, right next door to me, and I see the baby every day. Usually one of my kids goes over right away when we get home and brings her over. They all love the baby. Charles wanted to marry the girl, Hilda, but she wouldn't have him. I guess it's better this way—I can see it now. She has three or four boyfriends and Charles has a couple of girlfriends so it's better this way. Yeah, Hilda was real smart not to marry Charles; not that Charles is not a good man. But young kids now want to have a good time all the time, and not with one person. Nobody should get married too early."

Patricia Walker is always trying to get her mother to come up from Louisiana to stay with her, and her mother does come up on vacations, but she always goes back. She can't understand why anyone would actually want to live in Chicago.

However, the fact that her mother lives nearly a thousand miles away does not mean that they do not have an active relationship. Her son Henry, who is 18 years old, lives with his maternal grandmother in Louisiana during the year and comes up to Chicago during the summer to work. He is going to college next year and Patricia is very proud of this, knowing quite well what a difference it will make to his chances in life. The other big son dropped out of high school because he wanted to work, and her daughter Louise is on the verge of doing the same thing.

One could present much more detail on this case, but certain gross features are clear enough. The most striking thing is the strength and durability of the relationships among all these kinsfolk (and others not mentioned here). Take Patricia's father, for example. He left her mother when Patricia was less than one year old, but Patricia not only sees him regularly and is friendly with his current common-law wife, but she is concerned about his relatives, too. His sister, back in Louisiana, got sick recently, and it looked as though she might die. Patricia was in touch with her father frequently, by telephone, discussing when and how he would go down there, who would take care of the funeral arrangements, and so on. The father of her second and third children, Lawrence Tyler, she claims not to know as well as some of the others, but she is able to list a large number of his relatives, and observes that one of his brothers who lives in Cleveland is a real snooty type who thinks he is better than the rest of that family.

Patricia Walker, and countless women like her, is a living refutation of the idea that lower-class Afro-American kinship and family life is disorganized. She has enormous competence and self-confidence as a mother, and her ability to sustain relations with five men, fathers of her children, has nothing to do with "promiscuity," nor are the relationships imbued with the sexual significance which seems so prominent to many investigators. These men are fathers of her children, and she is linked to them by kinship ties through her children. She is a cheerful woman, not afraid of work, and certainly not given to feelings of personal inadequacy. On the contrary, she is secure in the knowledge that she knows how to cope with the world.

Patricia Walker's household is neither stably located geographically, nor in any sense independent. She and her children are connected and supported by myriad strands in a widespread network of kinship relations. None of her relatives could do a great deal for her in real adversity—those with the capacity to be a source of *real* help would probably minimize the tie—but she is in constant interaction with them and is clearly sustained by these relationships. Her mother comes and goes, she sends the children to visit their paternal grandmothers, she looks after her son's illegitimate child every day, and the fathers of her children keep in touch with her.

If Patricia Walker were in a stable, coresidential marital relationship with one of the fathers of her children, this would not signify a basic shift in family structure. The issue of stable coresidence is really much less crucial to an understanding of the normative structure of kinship and family relations than is supposed. Although the problem of economic support is important for women with children, and men need women to perform certain services for them, Patricia Walker's case demonstrates the manner in which it is possible to provide mutual services without stable coresidential conjugal unions.

Billingsley has pointed out that, in the United States, the majority of children of all classes are raised in two-parent, male-headed homes, and that the incidence of female-headed, one-parent homes increases markedly at the lower income levels. The clear implication is that "there is nothing like a good steady job with adequate and dependable income to make a man get married, stay married, remain with his family, and support it, while the absence of such economic viability is highly correlated with the refusal of men to insure the stability of their families." [3] There is no denying the accuracy of such an empirical observation, but the implications drawn from it are more questionable. The association between steady, adequate income and family stability is presented as though income made possible the attainment of stable family life while inadequate income prevents it. It would be more accurate to say that a man with a steady job and income is more likely to settle into a steady relationship with one woman, a relationship from which he expects love expressed through sexual satisfaction, and adequate care in the form of his meals on time, clean clothes, a decent home, and so on. In turn he provides support for the woman and her chil-

[3] Andrew Billingsley, *Black Families in White America* (Englewood Cliffs, N.J.: Prentice-Hall, Inc., 1968), p. 24.

dren. This seems to be an accurate description of much working-class family life, both Black and White.

Structurally, this is a situation entirely different from the "normal" middle-class family system. It would not be anomalous to find several other types of relatives as part of the household, for example. Whether or not the children belong to the male household head seems to make little difference in his relations with them. There is no culturally elaborated image of the wicked stepfather corresponding to that of the cruel stepmother. The reason is, of course, that the father is in any case a much less close and nurturant individual than the mother, and whether he is the child's real father or not seems almost unimportant.

Once a lower-class couple participate in a relationship involving sexual relations and the provision of reciprocal services and support, the liaison has a tendency to continue simply because it is a going concern in which the couple have a complex adjustment to each other and to the children. On the other hand, such relationships are easily disrupted by all kinds of external circumstances. The reason most frequently given by women for marital breakup is that the man was "running around" or turned out to be "no good." Just what it means for a woman to say that her marriage broke up because she couldn't stand her husband's "running around" with other women is not easy to determine. In one sense the statement may be taken at face value; the husband's infidelity is a breach of the marital relationship. However, the fact of sexual infidelity is probably less important than the systematic diversion of the husband's time, money, and affection.

Certain practical considerations are doubtless important in determining the action to be taken in any particular case. If a woman with children is unable to find work, does not have access to welfare payments, and has no relatives to fall back upon for help, she may be more tolerant of her husband's "running around." However, it is unrealistic to try to reduce marital behavior to the dimensions of a zero-sum game. There are numerous cases of women supporting unemployed husbands, women who are highly tolerant of marital infidelity, and women who prefer independence to being tied down to one man, no matter how exemplary his behavior as a husband. The one thing that is abundantly clear is that the marital relationship is not the basis of family structure in the way it is for the middle class, and that marital disruption does not give rise to a broken home. A broken home in the lower class would be one in which a mother abandoned her children, leaving them to be taken care of by the father.

Nothing receives more attention in the literature on lower-class kinship than the supposed problems of paternal deprivation. From a middle-class point of view, a household without a father is incomplete for many reasons. The mother is without a proper reference point for the social position of herself and her children, but, more importantly, there is a feeling of incompleteness because of the cultural definition of a normal family. Lower-class persons are well aware of these middle-class normative expectations; as we have pointed out, they share the general conception of the nuclear family as a structural unit out of which all kinship relations are differentiated. A child completely without a father would be an anomaly, but few lower-class children are fatherless. In all the interviews involved in our research we did not find any preoccupation with problems of paternal deprivation. Genealogical investigation shows that most children have knowledge of, and contact with, their father and his kin even when the parents do not live together. In fact, most children are raised in two-parent homes, as Billingsley points out. The most frequent complaint of husbandless mothers is that the children need a man to discipline them, though the presence of a father or stepfather in the household does not alter the general pattern of children's involvement in peer group activities.

Perhaps the most telling criticism of theories that posit a "vicious circle" of poverty—paternal deprivation–inadequate socialization–poverty—is the existence of arguments to the effect that the authoritarian structure of patriarchal families destroys initiative and leads to low achievement aspiration. For example, it has been argued that Mexican-American families are too "strongly integrated" and too patriarchal to produce males who will be oriented toward long-term goals involving deferment of gratification, and consequently there is a perpetuation of poverty.[4] It seems more likely that satisfactory explanations of the persistence of poverty are to be found in an analysis of the structure of the economy and the social system generally, and whatever relationship exists between socialization and economic success is less direct than these theories would suggest. A close study of the child-rearing practices of the upper class would probably be revealing in this respect.

Premarital Pregnancy

The distinctions made above can be used to throw light on the much-discussed problems of teen-age pregnancy, illegitimacy, and welfare dependency. The first issue on which to be absolutely clear is that motherhood is an important part of female sex-role identity at all class levels in American society, but it is particularly important for the lower class as part of the bundle of attributes which define femaleness. For the developing lower-class girl it is the full adoption of female attributes which signal maturity; having boyfriends, having sexual intercourse, getting married, and having babies are all part of the demonstration of maturity.

Illegitimacy occurs at all social class levels. However, even allowing for the greater incidence of abortion and concealment among the middle and upper class, it is clear that lower-class girls tend to experience sexual intercourse at an earlier age and experience a higher rate of pre-marital pregnancy, primarily, we think, because of these differences in definition of sex-role. Another set of factors is also of importance in understanding the different class incidence of illegitimacy. For the middle class, illegitimacy is anomalous in relation to the normative stress upon the nuclear family as the proper setting for sexual relations and child-rearing, and the position of the child in the status system is anomalous. The normal middle-class reaction to illegitimate pregnancy is to terminate the pregnancy or to assimilate the child to a "normal" family situation

---

[4] See Leo Grebler, Joan W. Moore, and Ralph C. Guzman, *The Mexican-American People* (New York: The Free Press, 1970), p. 369.

by hasty marriage or placing it with a carefully selected adopting family.

The lower-class context is quite different. While any American female will experience a sense of shame, regret, or distress at bearing a child conceived outside a relationship which involves love and a measure of social approval, the situation of the child is not anomalous in the same way that it is for the middle class. The status factor is less influential, for the simple reason that illegitimacy, while it may carry a measure of stigma, cannot act as a major status depressant. Most important is the fact that the child can be assimilated to a normal family which does not have to be an independent nuclear family. This is not to say that there will not be problems of support, health, and so on, but they are problems which would exist if the child were born within the framework of a legal union. The social problems of welfare dependency cannot be equated with problems of family structure or illegitimacy; they exist in their own right and, like poverty itself, are an integral part of the structure of American society as it is now constituted.

Much of the recent concern about illegitimacy in the United States has focused on the supposed pathological condition of the "Negro family." The Moynihan Report[5] represents a distillation of ideas which were in wide circulation even though the report expresses them in a much more plausible and systematic way. Without suggesting that the Moynihan Report is simply an expression of these particular ideas, one can perhaps characterize them in the following way. The working population of the United States is forced to pay taxes, part of which go to support an increasing number of children through the Aid to Families of Dependent Children (AFDC) scheme. This procedure was originated to continue the help given to widows and orphans by the various Mother's Aid schemes, but it has increasingly come to be used to support families which have been abandoned by the father, and increasingly these families are Black. It is pointed out that illegitimacy rates are higher

[5] More properly referred to as *The Negro Family: The Case for National Action* (Washington, D.C.: Office of Policy Planning and Research, United States Department of Labor, 1965).

among Blacks than among Whites, that many Black women have more than one illegitimate child, and that many illegitimate children end up on AFDC rolls. It is not a difficult logical step to the idea that, if Black families could be rescued from "the tangle of pathology" into which they have fallen, one could not only solve the problems of Black concentration in the lower class—because children would be brought up with the right motives to enable them to enter steady employment after proper schooling—but one would also do away with the "immorality" which illegitimacy represents, and also save the taxpayers money, which may be the most important consideration of all.

Merely stating this supposed solution to the problems of racialism and poverty is almost enough to show how ludicrous it actually is. Bloomberg and Schmandt put the position quite well when they say: ". . . our failure [to reduce impoverishment] is a product, not so much of ignorance or of individual intransigence, but mainly of the very fabric of our social system, our institutions, our political arrangements. By the time one reaches the end of this book it is sadly clear that the poverty we deplore issues from the same source as many of the pleasures enjoyed by those who have written its various chapters and by the varied readers who may consult its contents." [6] They go on to point out that the world inhabited by the urban poor is not some "other America" but an integral, perhaps necessary, part of the America of affluence known to the middle class.

One final observation may be made in regard to ethnicity and to the other internal differentiations within the lower class which give rise to the conception of a working class. The position of Afro-Americans in the United States is a matter of considerable national importance which has been the focus of attention for sociologists and anthropologists for well over a decade now. There is no ignoring the singularity of the predicament of Black people when they are faced with a racialism which compounds the problems of poverty. However, the lower class in America is by no means exclusively

[6] W. Bloomberg, and H. J. Schmandt, eds., *Power, Poverty, and Urban Policy,* Urban Affairs Annual Reviews, Vol. 2 (Beverly Hills, Cal.: Sage Publications Inc., 1968), p. 10.

Black, and Black people are certainly not exclusively lower class. There is some evidence that the struggles of Blacks against racial discrimination and economic exploitation are generating similar movements in other ethnic groups, movements which often take on the appearance of resentment against Blacks but which contain the potential for a broad class movement, particularly in the cities. So far as family structure is concerned, it seems to us that the patterns prevalent among poor Blacks, which are sometimes depicted as being peculiarly Afro-American, are in fact class-based and not ethnically distinct.

Just as ethnicity does not constitute a useful index to variation in family structure among those most subject to poverty and insecurity of income, so it does not serve as a means of distinguishing a working class. The majority of the lower class are fairly steadily employed wage earners, and while racist policies and practices in the trade unions, residential patterns, and so on, have made it difficult for Blacks in the past, they now constitute an increasing proportion of the steadily employed working class. Irrespective of ethnicity, the stabilization of employment and earning power for men appears to have a stabilizing effect upon marital relations. This does not mean that normative family structure becomes the same as middle class, for the content of the marital relationship remains different, and it is contained within a different overall family pattern.

We are totally opposed to the idea of class and ethnic subcultures as bundles of discrete cultural traits to be counterposed against a similar bundle of American "common values." Subcultural elements are in a constant process of creation and re-creation in the interaction among basic modes of understanding, more concretized models for action, and the experience of the world as it presents itself in practice. To refer to middle-class normative structures as "normal" or "mainstream" or "societal" is merely to restate a basic fact about the locus of power in American society. Lower-class people are aware of the practical "superiority" of middle-class norms, but they also know, in an equally practical way, that they are not themselves middle-class, and that their family and kinship relations are not in any sense pathological.

CONCLUSION

Chapter 8

Our central concerns in this book have been two. First, we have attempted to understand the nature of differences in family structure and kinship behavior within American society. We chose "class" as the most significant basis of variation, partly because our data made this a necessary choice, partly because of our more inclusive view of the structure and development of American society in particular and of complex industrial societies in general. Second, our primary theoretical concern has been an attempt actually to work out, in as systematic a manner as possible, the relationship among culture, normative or social system, and social action. The problem with treating culture at such high levels of generality as appear to be analytically necessary raises the problem of how such highly general symbols and meanings can be shown to relate to concrete patterns of behavior. We have aimed in this book to refute the criticism that culture, in the way in which we have used the concept, is so far removed from behavior as to be useless in its understanding or analysis.

In this final chapter we draw together the main threads of our argument by first providing a summary of the major issues which have been presented, and then by a further discussion of the concept of class and its relevance to the analysis of modern society.

We begin with the observation that most sociological and

anthropological investigations of the family, in this and in other societies, start from certain assumptions about the nature of kinship which, while purporting to be objective or universally valid, actually reflect Euro-American cultural conceptions. We have considered it important to examine our informant's conceptions about the nature of kinship, sex, the family, and allied aspects of social life, since we believe that these conceptions are themselves an important part of any objective study. In our analysis we found it profitable to distinguish:

1. Cultural conceptions of a very general order which are often taken for granted and assumed to be "obvious" facts about the way things "really are." We believe that these conceptions are relatively stable over long periods of time, but because they are formulated at a high level of generality they are thereby invested with varying meanings and are transformed into more specific rules to fit a range of differing situations. The assumption that "blood" is transmitted to the child by both parents, and that the possession of common blood creates indestructible relationships between individuals, is a general conception of this kind. Specification of the ideal content of such relationships varies considerably with time and social situation.[1]

2. Normative structures. These function to guide both perception and action in real social interactive situations and contain, among other things, conglomerations of elements drawn from a number of different cultural domains. Normative rules may be specified in many different ways, ranging from precise legal forms to more variable, and sometimes vague, statements about what is the right thing to do under given circumstances. Because normative structures function in situations of social interaction they are responsive to feedback from experience, and are precise only in proportion to the distance they are removed from particular action contexts.

---

[1] We do not deal here with the question of how changes take place in these general conceptions, nor do we explore the question of the range within which derived norms can vary while still being integrally related to the general cultural concept.

3. Patterns of actual behavior, which are the resultant of a number of interacting forces. It is easy to confuse observed regularities of behavior with normative patterns, especially since the two must meet in the existential moment of action, but they cannot be treated as identical. Patterns of behavior are affected by ecological and demographic factors and by the exigencies of social system functioning. Ultimately such forces will, or may, impress themselves upon normative patterns, but those patterns must still be distinguished as separate analytical elements in the structure of social action.

One of the paradoxical findings of social science research on the family in the United States is that there is considerable variation in behavior, much of it apparently associated with differences in status and/or economic condition, but at the same time there appears to be considerable uniformity in the degree to which people value marriage and what is frequently defined as a normal family life. Of course it is often difficult to ascertain just what these values are and the extent to which they are simply statements of the respondent's knowledge of the most prestigious normative structures. It is also frequently difficult to determine the conditions under which value statements were elicited. On the assumption that there was a definite uniformity of values accompanied by variations in behavior, sundry devices have been introduced to bridge the gap between supposed values and actual behavior. The concept of the "lower class value stretch" [2] seems to have retained its appeal for many years, as evidenced by its recent use by Rainwater,[3] but all it does is restate the facts in a slightly different form.

It is our contention that the distinctions we have made provide a much better basis for the discussion of variation in American family structure, and they have certainly provided us with a much

---

[2] Hyman Rodman, "The Lower Class Value Stretch," *Social Forces*, 42 (December 1963), pp. 205–215.

[3] Lee Rainwater, *Behind Ghetto Walls* (Chicago: Aldine-Atherton, 1970), pp. 365–366.

better understanding of our own field data. The situation, so far as variation in kinship and family structure is concerned, can be summarized as follows:

1. At the level of pure cultural conceptions in the domain of kinship, there is no variation of any detectable significance. The same fundamental assumptions about the nature of kinship and the relations generated by marriage occur in our interviews from both middle and lower class. Americans of all classes share the same conceptions about the manner in which "blood" is transmitted and the imperishable bonds it creates between people. Americans of all classes define fatherhood and motherhood in the same way at this general level: the father is the man whose semen fertilized the ovum in a particular woman, and the mother is the woman who bore the child. Also at this level, "marriage" means something like "united by love into a socially sanctioned union"; there is considerable room for variation in the manner in which such a union shall be institutionalized. It is clear that, at this cultural level, the biological premises and assumptions, and indeed the biological elements themselves, are symbols which stand for a particular kind of relationship among those who are said to be related in those ways, and that is a relationship of diffuse, enduring solidarity. It is a mistake to assume that statements which appear to be about biology, semen and the fertilization of the egg, and the nature of "blood" are literally about these things. Rather, they stand for the unity which persons so related are supposed to have, about the ability of each to depend without qualification on the other, about their love (which means both enduring affection and coitus) for each other, and about the enduring quality of that relation of solidarity. It goes without saying that whether or not the biological relations do actually exist is irrelevant to and independent of their symbolic, cultural meaning.

At this level, each person in his capacity as a relative or kinsman is equal to each other relative, and undifferentiated from him. It is not that a father and a mother, a son and a daughter are relatives; all are equally relatives without regard to age, sex, or generation, and each has the same relationship of diffuse enduring solidarity to every other relative. In this respect the unit resembles what Durkheim has called one of "mechanical solidarity." [4]

The same biological symbols apply at the next level, the level at which the family members are differentiated precisely in terms of their biological characteristics as male and female, older and younger. At this cultural level we may also say that Americans share a conception of "the nuclear family" as the basic configuration of kinship elements out of which the whole domain of kinship is defined and differentiated. The unit of father and mother, and the children produced by their union in an act of love, is clearly a basic paradigm for conceptualizing kinship relations generally. This unit is organized so as to approximate what Durkheim called one of "organic solidarity," [5] in that each member of the unit is differentiated in particular terms, and his existence as an element in the total unit is predicated both on his differentiation and his interdependence with every other part of the unit. The father fertilizes the egg, the mother bears the egg and the child it becomes, and the child is the outcome of the act of coitus or love between the parents. The child is dependent on the parents and will, when adult, repay that dependence, and so on.

It is worth noting that, within this same paradigm and within the same meanings of the basic biological symbols involved, the relationship between male and female, husband and wife, mother and father, son and daughter, brother and sister within the family can be one of sex equality or inequality. The characteristic of inequality or equality is not *necessarily* inherent in the biological definitions which constitute the cultural symbols. The argument for each position can be made on precisely the same biological grounds. That women are inferior to men can be a reasonable inference from their child-bearing and child-rearing biological functions, while the argument that they are different but equal can be made on precisely the same grounds. That there has been, over the past few hundred years, a process of dedifferentiation and redifferentiation in the roles

---

[4] Emile Durkheim, *The Division of Labor in Society*, trans. by G. Simpson (Glencoe, Ill. The Free Press, 1947), Chap. 2.

[5] Durkheim, *The Division of Labor in Society*, Chap. 3.

of men and women in terms of equality and in the basic cultural conception of equality in biological terms is self-evident to most students of the subject.

2. There is a definite variation in the structuring of the norms which provide rules for the formation of real families and for the proper relations which should govern the behavior of family members toward each other. These variations seem to follow class lines, and they have a complex relation to ethnicity. At this level norms are rules for behavior which specify the proper modes of action for persons who are differentiated in a number of distinct domains. For example, a person who plays the role of "mother" in a family is at the same time playing the role of "woman" (though it is not unknown for men to act as "mothers" in one sense of the term), she also has a role in the class system, she may fill an occupational role, and so on. We argue that normative role structures for family members vary precisely because they are conglomerate structures of this kind, and the most important dimension of variation is in the class differences in sex-role. Over and above these variations in the sex-role component of familial norms is a peculiarity of the middle class which needs to be stressed. It is a feature of middle-class normative structure that the nuclear family itself, as a unit, is singled out for special emphasis. The family, meaning the independent unit of husband, wife, and children, is personified and treated as a unique area of solidarity within the kinship domain. Neither the lower class nor the upper class place the same emphasis upon a restricted and independent nuclear family unit, but instead see the family as assuming a more flexible form. Empirically, of course, one finds nuclear families as the most frequent coresidential units at all class levels, but this should not be viewed as the result of the implementation of some abstract ideal of "normal" family life. For the middle class, an independent nuclear family built around the income of the husband/father is indeed both an ideal and a highly functional unit within the system of occupational and status mobility. For the lower class, the existence of nuclear family units represents the conjunction of conjugal and child-rearing activities, but does not preclude continuation of strong functional relationships across the

boundaries of the unit, or ready acceptance of other forms of co-residential unit when circumstances demand. ⟨Perhaps the major difference between middle- and lower-class familial normative structure lies in the fact that sex-roles vary quite sharply. Whereas in the middle class there is an emphasis for both sexes upon the value of performance according to rational criteria in tasks which are decreasingly sex-linked, the lower-class emphasis is upon the sharply differing qualities which are believed to inhere in maleness or femaleness.⟩Whereas the middle class lay emphasis upon the relationship between men and women as being one of loving intercourse in which the relationship itself is stressed above the particular form it may take, in the lower class the relationship between men and women is based upon a clear distinction of fields of activity which are complementary but sharply segregated. These differences are reflected in the nature of conjugal relations, and of course they reveal themselves in processes of socialization and maturation.⟨For the middle-class child, "growing up" means increasing mastery over rational techniques, and there is minimal differentiation between males and females in this process of education;[6] for the lower-class child, "growing up" means learning to be a man or a woman and exhibiting the qualities of masculinity and femininity which are clearly defined and differentiated.⟩

3. There is considerable variation in behavior, and such variation is continuous within and between social classes. Variation in behavior is not simply the expression of cultural conceptions or of normative structures; it is affected by a great many other factors, such as we outlined in Chapter 7. Variations in behavior are necessarily measured in quantitative terms, and can be expressed quite precisely and accurately if the initial observations are accurate. However, it is easy to draw mistaken inferences from statistics showing rates of behavior. For example, the frequency of occurrence of households of a particular configuration should not be used as a means for arriving at conclusions about what is normal in other than a statistical sense. Such factors as variation in the availability

---

[6] The argument is somewhat simplified, of course, and we are not unaware of the considerable residue of attributional difference in middle-class sex-roles.

of housing units can affect household composition. One of the most important sets of forces affecting familial behavior is the relationship of individuals and families to the economic system. Steady employment for males, with involvement in a range of welfare plans such as medical and unemployment insurance, savings and life insurance, and home purchase schemes, provide a stabilizing effect upon marriage and reinforce middle-class normative stress upon the nuclear family. Unemployment and irregular employment, coupled with high rates of female participation in the labor market, has the opposite effect. In neither case is this relationship to economic factors determinative in any simple way of familial structure at the behavioral level. For the lower class it often results in the emergence of the perfectly normal configuration of domestic units based on a stable female core, to which males are related in a variety of supportive, dominant, or dependent ways.

Class and the Value of Rationality in Modern Society

The model of middle-class kinship and family structure presented in Chapter 4 stressed the importance of rationality as the basis for decision making and the major guide for behavior. It appears that technical, or logical, rules for solving problems, acquired by the learning of general skills, have come to replace socially derived and behavior-specific norms acquired by a process of role internalization. Rather than a dramaturgical view of social action, we now see individual and social behavior as predominantly determined by the application of technical rules to any situation that arises. In order to understand social action, it appears that we must understand the generalized rules, the "structure," which actors apply to the solution of existential "problems."

To this model we contrasted a lower-class pattern of more traditional orientation in which authority, sex-role differentiation, and kinship solidarities are suffused with moral significance predicated on the particularities of the roles and their intersubjective relations.

It is no accident that our two models display a polarity of this nature. Jürgen Habermas has pointed out that all the paired concepts such as:

> Status and contract, Gemeinschaft and Gesellschaft, mechanical and organic solidarity, informal and formal groups, primary and secondary groups, culture and civilization, traditional and bureaucratic authority, sacral and secular associations, military and industrial society, status group and class— all of these represent as many attempts to grasp the structural change of the institutional framework of a traditional society on the way to becoming a modern one. Even Parsons' catalog of possible alternatives of value-orientations belongs in the list of these attempts, although he would not admit it.[7]

Of course the United States is not simply a "traditional society on the way to becoming a modern one"; it is the most modern of all existing societies, with the most advanced degree of rationalization in the sense in which Weber used that concept.[8] As a detached colonial society, created in the recent historical past, it was in an excellent position to proceed to the full development of "rational bourgeois capitalism" unhampered by traditional social and political institutions.[9] Despite the problem of absorbing large numbers of migrants from Europe and elsewhere, and the bitter struggles of the working class against the most brutal forms of exploitation in the early stages of industrialization, the idea of scientific–technical principles came to be applied to industrial management, labor relations, government, and indeed the whole of social life at a relatively early stage.[10] However, the conscious amelioration of class conflict

---

[7] Jürgen Habermas, *Toward a Rational Society* (Boston: Beacon Press, 1970), pp. 90–91.

[8] See Max Weber, *The Theory of Social and Economic Organization* (Glencoe, Ill.: The Free Press, 1947).

[9] See S. M. Lipset, *The First New Nation* (New York: Basic Books, Inc., Publishers, 1963); T. Parsons, *The System of Modern Societies* (Englewood Cliffs, N.J.: Prentice-Hall, Inc., 1971); L. Harz, *The Founding of New Societies* (New York: Harcourt Brace Jovanovich, Inc., 1964).

[10] See, for example, Elton Mayo, *The Social Problems of an Industrial Civilization* (Boston: Harvard University Graduate School of Business Administration 1945); D. Bell, *Work and Its Discontents: The Cult of Efficiency in America* (Boston: Beacon Press, 1956).

through trade union action and government intervention is still relatively recent; it was the existence of a more extensive opportunity structure, first through frontier expansion and then through high levels of industrial expansion, that inhibited the emergence of a sharply defined and conscious class structure. Doubtless the ideology of egalitarianism had some influence as well.

Over the past 40 years or so—since the New Deal—there has been a progressive intensification of the trends already present. In the economic sphere the techniques of mass production and mass marketing, leading to mass consumption, have spread in an unprecedented manner. Trade unions have become entrenched to the point where they are an integral part of the system of productive relations, and unionization has been spreading into white collar, technical, and even professional groups. The educational system has become the principal instrument for the legitimation of status aspirations through progressive "diplomatization" as the basis for entry to occupations. The universities are major research centers crucial to the maintenance of the social system and the future growth of the economy.[11] The federal government has taken an increasingly active role in regulation of the economy and provision of minimal levels of welfare. Under these circumstances, there appears to have been a considerable increase in the size of the middle class—as measured by income and ability to consume—and a concomitant change in the shape of the income pyramid into something more like a diamond-shaped distribution.[12]

If present trends continue, the line between middle class and working class will undoubtedly become increasingly blurred as the *embourgeoisement* of the workers proceeds, and class conflict of any significant kind will disappear. The major social problems will then reside in the extension of adequate levels of welfare to all sections of the population.[13] An important element in these developments

[11] See J. Ben-David, *The Sociology of Science* (Englewood Cliffs, N.J.: Prentice-Hall, Inc., 1971).
[12] See Kurt Mayer, "The Changing Shape of the American Class Structure," *Social Research*, 30 (1963), pp. 458–468.
[13] See John H. Goldthorpe, David Lockwood, Frank Bechhofer, and Jennifer Platt, *The Affluent Worker in the Class Structure* (Cambridge: Cambridge Univer-

is the changing character of blue collar occupations arising from the increasing emphasis upon cooperative, technically guided relations between management and worker, in place of the old relations of authority based upon the power of the management to terminate the worker's employment.

We are in no position to assess the extent of these supposed changes, but it is important to our argument to consider just what social matrix is necessary for continuation of the pattern of family structure we labeled "lower class," what consequences might flow from the progressive rationalization of life styles, and whether the movement is not toward an extension of the middle-class pattern and the transformation of the traditional lower-class pattern into a truly disorganized version of the middle class, thus actualizing the picture now drawn by the bulk of social science writing on lower-class and poverty populations. We must also assess the effect of increasing rationalization upon the new working class, and judge whether the image of a new integrated capitalist welfare state is accurate or likely to become so in the future.

The Social Basis
of Lower-Class Kinship

The traditional lower- and working-class population not only filled subordinate, and frequently insecure, positions in the occupational system, but also lived in neighborhoods where there was some continuity of residence (with a consequent accumulation of kinship and neighborhood ties), and a measure of community life which involved people in networks of relationship extending beyond the immediate family. Such working-class communities could contain a range of degrees of success or failure, with resources being redistributed through kinship networks, and with everyone contained

sity Press, 1969); Habermas, *Toward a Rational Society*; John K. Galbraith, *The New Industrial State* (Boston: Houghton Mifflin Company, 1967); Robert Blauner, *Alienation and Freedom: The Factory Worker and His Industry* (Chicago: University of Chicago Press, 1964).

within a tradition-oriented way of life. Communities of this kind have been well documented for Britain, and less well so for the United States.[14]

Such communities take time to become established, and in their initial stages often appear to be (and frequently are) disorganized and unstable. Modern inner city slums occupied mainly by Black populations have some special characteristics, but for all their current disorganization they continue to produce some of the typical community structure of traditional working-class neighborhoods. This is even more true of the more prosperous areas of Black urban settlement, where there is a higher incidence of home ownership. The pattern of extreme localization of ties, such as found in the East End of London, is less likely to exist in modern American cities with their high rise apartments and multiple-family buildings, but this does not mean that networks of kinship and friendship relations do not proliferate in the same way. Although it is common to use the term "ghetto" as a general reference to the "Black belts" of the inner cities, and while racial discrimination in housing forces a concentration of Blacks and pushes people of varying socioeconomic status into closer contact than might otherwise be the case, there are marked variations within these Black belts. In Chicago, for example, there is a great deal of difference between the Public Housing projects, which contain a high proportion of families on welfare, and the more prosperous areas of South Shore, where Black families have been moving into areas of well-kept single family homes, or the blocks of new housing further south in the area of 95th Street east of Ashland Avenue.

Quite apart from the growth of these areas of lower middle-

---

[14] See, for example, Michael Willmott and Peter Young, *Family and Kinship in East London* (London: Routledge & Kegan Paul, 1957); J. M. Mogey, *Family and Neighbourhood* (Oxford: Oxford University Press, 1956); Colin Rosser and Christopher Harris,*The Family and Social Change* (London: Routledge & Kegan Paul, 1965); M. Stacey, *Tradition and Change: A Study of Banbury* (Oxford: Oxford University Press, 1960). For the U.S. see Herbert Gans, *The Urban Villagers* (New York: The Free Press, 1962), and *The Levittowners* (New York: Pantheon, 1967); Bennett Berger, *Working Class Suburb* (Berkeley: University of California Press, 1960); W. Lloyd Warner and Paul S. Lunt, *The Status System of a Modern Community* (New Haven: Yale University Press, 1941).

class and working-class Black housing, one finds many cases in which extended families of Blacks have developed and persisted through many generations of increasing economic success in northern cities. The persistence of these localized kinship groups may result from the difficulties faced by Blacks when they try to move into higher status white neighborhoods, so that the economically more successful are forced to stay in the same locality. We have discovered several such extended family groups—in places like Evanston, Illinois —and have reports of others from such cities as Detroit and its suburbs.

It would be incorrect to suggest that there is a constant and uniform tendency toward the stabilization of the lower-class, disorganized urban population; obviously the peculiarities and imperfections of a competitive, unplanned economy produce varying forms of dislocation. Individuals may become almost completely detached from meaningful relationship networks and drift into alcoholism, drug addiction, prostitution, or other forms of criminal activity. In an earlier day the "hobo" problem was just as acute, and was produced by the demand for casual migratory labor to work on the westward expansion of the railroads and other frontier activities. Chicago in the first decades of the nineteenth century was the headquarters of "hobohemia," posing problems just as acute as the welfare problems of today.[15]

Working- and lower-class traditionalism is not simply a residue of the past—a persistence into the city of a rural, small-community way of life. It is rather the specific creation of urban conditions, clearly shown in the emphasis upon money income and the forms of mutual assistance which draw kinsfolk together. Its basis seems to be position in a system of relations of economic production, a position involving low income, low status, and vulnerability to unemployment, which in turn generates feelings of insecurity. Writings on the condition of the English working classes in the early period of industrialization tended to emphasize disorganization, dis-

---

[15] See Nels Anderson, *The Hobo* (Chicago: The University of Chicago Press, 1923), and David M. Schneider, *The History of Public Welfare in New York State, 1867–1940* (Chicago: The University of Chicago Press, 1941).

solution of familial and kinship ties, and degeneration of morals in a manner similar to much of the recent writing on American society.[16] However, it was in those urban areas of England that stable working-class communities developed. The industrial areas of Lancashire, Yorkshire, the Midlands, and East London, which have been depicted in more recent studies of working-class culture, were at one time the subject of the study of disorganization. In the United States the process was quite similar, but the constant influx of immigrants into the lowest status occupations has tended to produce a feeling of movement, mobility, and status enhancement, no matter how small it may have been in reality. The exception to this generalization has been the experience of the Blacks who, until very recently, had every real or attempted advance turned back.

The Differentiation of the Middle Class

Since World War II there has been an increasing awareness, in both Europe and the United States, of the effect of higher wages and higher living standards upon the social life and class identification of the more skilled or more regularly employed sections of the working class. The question has been raised—as we indicated earlier—as to whether the old working class is not being increasingly absorbed into an expanding middle class, leaving behind only a lumpenproletariat of unemployed, and largely unemployable, outsiders.

Even a superficial examination is sufficient to cast doubt on these propositions. We took as being central to our model of middle-class rationality the idea of "competence," particularly the competence necessary for making a success of a life's career. While it could be argued that it is the upper middle, rather than the generality of the middle class, that is career-oriented and preoccupied

---

[16] See P. Gaskell, *Artisans and Machinery* (London: John W. Parker, 1836); F. Engels, *The Condition of the Working Class in England* (Stanford, Calif.: Stanford University Press, 1968).

with both competence and the application of rationality principles to an ever-widening range of activities, we shall assume this to be a central feature of the model we have labeled "middle-class." In the occupational sphere, competence implies a measure of control by the individual in the shaping of the enterprise in which he is concerned, and leaves at least a minimal opportunity for the exercise of creative ability. It is true that the physician or the factory manager is largely concerned with the application of technical procedures to the solution of newly developing problems, but each one has the opportunity to shape such application in varying ways, with his success being measured not only by the absence of error, but also by the extent of innovation. Despite the rewards of conformity described by such writers as Riesman and Whyte,[17] there is at least some expectation of "progress" in the development of innovative technique.

None of this applies to the occupational activities of the blue collar working class or to the lower echelons of clerical and technical white collar workers. For them it is no less true today than it was when Adam Smith wrote, that "The man whose life is spent in performing a few simple operations . . . has no occasion on which to exert his understanding." However, whether "he generally becomes as stupid and ignorant as it is possible for a human creature to become"[18] is another, more complex, question. The increased rationalization of work procedures leads first to the development of what Bell has called the logics of size, time, and hierarchy, where work is concentrated in large assembly areas, reduced to standardized motions measured in ever more precise and smaller time units, and arranged in hierarchical systems such that

> modern industry has had to devise an entirely new managerial superstructure which organizes and directs production. This

[17] David Riesman, *The Lonely Crowd* (New Haven: Yale University Press, 1951); William H. Whyte, *The Organization Man* (New York: Simon & Schuster Inc., 1956).

[18] Adam Smith, *Wealth of Nations*, quoted in Bell, *Work and Its Discontents*, p. 7.

superstructure draws all possible brainwork away from the shop; everything is centered in the planning and schedule and design departments. And in this new hierarchy there stands a figure known neither to the handicrafts nor to industry in its infancy—the technical employee. With him, the separation of functions becomes complete. The worker at the bottom, attending only to a detail, is divorced from any decision or modification about the product he is working on.[19]

We see the paradoxical situation of workers becoming more dissatisfied as the structure of production becomes more rational, and increased consumption becoming the only satisfaction to be found in work. The evidence for this is now overwhelming, and comes from Europe as well as from the United States.[20] The situation is not markedly different in the lower levels of the white collar occupations, where workers are increasingly reduced to the performance of simple repetitive tasks requiring neither initiative nor thought.

In what way does this work situation react upon family life, and can it be considered a key factor in the structuring of kinship roles? It has been suggested that the progressive *embourgeoisement* of the working class is to be sought not in the nature of their work, or their relation to the means of production, but in the style of life made possible by steadily rising incomes and consumption power. However, as numerous writers have shown, a convergence in either incomes or consumption power does not in itself imply a convergence in life styles, and we share the view that there continues to be a world of difference between the typical style of life of the upper middle class (often referred to as "the liberals" by blue collar workers) and that of the working class. Naturally there is considerable variation among particular families, especially where mobility orientations have been sufficient to produce real movement on the part of the children, and it is possible to make the kind of classification presented by Gans when he speaks of the "restrictive" and

---

[19] Bell, *Work and Its Discontents*, p. 10.

[20] See J. H. Goldthorpe, *et al.*, *The Affluent Worker: Industrial Attitudes and Behaviour* (Cambridge: Cambridge University Press, 1968).

"expansive" subgroups of the lower middle class, or the "conservative–managerial" or "liberal–professional" segments of the upper middle class.[21] There is no end to such categorization, and although there is a pervasive *general* orientation toward social mobility in American society, and an increasingly realistic appreciation of the value of education as a means of breaking away from parental status, the amount and the range of such mobility has limits. These limits effectively inhibit the development in the working and lower middle class of the pervasively rationalizing orientation of the upper levels of the middle class. The mobility orientations of the working class are expressed either through an increase in the sheer quantity of work, which will then permit higher consumption levels, or in the faith that a frugal and traditionally moral way of life (Gans' "restrictive" category) will be rewarded by some higher power.

Thus we conclude that the models which we developed in the body of this monograph are more useful to our purposes than a highly elaborated series of special subgroups of the broadly conceived class groupings. We further conclude that the broad distinction drawn between a rational orientation to the world and a more traditional orientation is a valid part of these models, despite the general, or encompassing, rationality which pervades the system as a whole.

On this latter issue we agree with such writers as Marcuse and Habermas, who contend that the scientific–rational characterization of American society, which tends to present value problems as technical problems, is itself an ideology linked to a specific form of political domination. As Marcuse says:

> In the medium of technology, culture, politics, and the economy merge into an omnipresent system which swallows up or repulses all alternatives. The productivity and growth potential of this system stabilize the society and contain technical progress within the framework of domination. Technological rationality has become political rationality.[22]

[21] Gans, *The Levittowners*, pp. 29–31.
[22] Herbert Marcuse, *One-Dimensional Man* (Boston: Beacon Press, 1964), p. xvi.

It has been suggested that the progressive rationalization of productive processes, and eventually of the whole of society, is the specific achievement of a new managerial class which has gradually supplanted the old owner–managerial class, and in the process has altered existing hierarchies of power, prestige, and status. The idea of the salience of such a class goes back to St. Simon and Fourier; in more recent times it was revived by James Burnham.[23] Whether the managers have successfully supplanted older dominant classes is a moot point, but what is clear is the extent to which the managerial group is self-recruited (irrespective of the nature of the type of political system involved), and therefore the extent to which it constitutes a class with certain interests in societal domination.[24] Postan shows that, in both Britain and France, the "new managerial class" blended imperceptibly into the existing upper layers of society, rather than instituting a radical break with the past, even though the business executive has an orientation to organization, efficiency, and power which is quite different from that of the traditional upper class.

To sum up this discussion of the differentiation within the middle class, we might say that the group which approximates our model most closely is the upper middle class of managerial and executive elites, whose political interests are closely merged with those of the upper class and the older "tycoon" capitalist groups. Their occupational milieu is the controlling and decision-making levels of firms and governmental bureaucracies. The lower middle class appears to be merging with the upper levels of the lower or working class into what has variously been called the New Working Class or an expanded middle class, the ranks of which are swollen by the addition of bourgeoisified manual workers. There is heated debate as to whether this new working class represents the unstable focus of the contradictions within capitalism, and will thus be the vanguard of a new order, or is the stable core of an

[23] James Burnham, *The Managerial Revolution* (New York: John Day Co., 1941).
[24] See M. M. Postan, *An Economic History of Western Europe 1945–1964* (London: Methuen, 1967); pp. 265–345 contain some interesting comparative discussion of Europe, the U.S., and the U.S.S.R.

increasingly integrated and rationalized postcapitalist social order. We agree with Lockwood and his fellow authors that these are questions for sociological investigation rather than dogmatic assertion.[25] It seems to us that it is within this sector of the society that the multiplicity of variations between our two general models can best be studied, and where the relationship between the components of the models can be clarified. For example, if there is a process of increasing rationalization within the general orientation of the upper levels of the lower class, how will it work out in social system terms? Can lower-class family life take on the characteristics of the upper-middle-class model without the possibility of pervasive change in occupational and other domains? This is only another way of asking how cultural codes interact with other factors, or the extent to which they can be considered to be in any way independent of the other aspects of social action.

Elizabeth Bott has dealt with some of the factors that have been discussed in this monograph.[26] She argued that variations in the internal structuring of familial roles, particularly the relationship between husband and wife, depend on such factors as stability of residence in local communities and the consequent degree of connectedness of external networks, rather than varying directly according to class factors. The existence of such intervening variables is an important consideration which further complicates analysis, especially when one adopts the kind of intensive study of small samples used by Bott and by ourselves. But we believe that there are systematic differences in normative structure between classes which derive not only from the instrumental aspects of social roles, but also from the cultural or evaluative aspects of differential orientations and their application to action in the world of social behavior.

The rational orientation which we referred to in the model of middle-class kinship norms is not the same as a rationalized pattern

---

[25] Lockwood *et al.*, *The Affluent Worker in the Class Structure*, p. 28.

[26] Elizabeth Bott, *Family and Social Network* (London: Tavistock Publications Ltd., 1956).

of behavior as set out by a work study engineer. Indeed, to behave in a totally rationalized manner permits neither the application of rationality norms to a choice between alternative courses of action, nor the satisfying embellishment provided by traditional encrustation. Furthermore, the process of rationalization within industrial–capitalist society assumes that the ultimate ends are given in the form of basic cultural premises about individualism and the emergence of a just social order through the interplay of the rationally-oriented interests of individual actors.

Needless to say, such cultural assumptions either originate as the ideology of a controlling class, or are shaped out of earlier elements during the process of social domination. The extent to which they are deeply rooted in the society at large is an index to the efficiency (the legitimation) of the domination.

We have pointed out that rationality is a dominant value of the whole system, and to that extent legitimation has been accomplished. Middle-class rationality, we said, is harnessed to the attempt to control the world, while lower-class rationality is concerned with the maximization of security within an unpredictable and largely uncontrollable social world. If lower-class rationality were to be shifted in its orientation so that traditionalism was increasingly effaced in favor of a more activist, revolutionary (that is, middle-class), direction, then it would inevitably result in the attempt to change the present system of domination, and involve the questioning of the very ends to which middle-class rationalism is devoted. There are many indications of such shifts on a small scale in modern American life, but not of the magnitude that would lead one to believe that any dramatic restructuring of the society is imminent. The major problem for the new working-cum-lower middle class, and for the lower class, is to avoid social atomization, whether it be in the new suburban housing tracts in California or in the projects and tenements of the inner cities.

For the present kinship provides the most powerful defense against such atomization, just as for the middle class it provides a counterbalance to the demand for constant maintenance of technical achievement. To the extent that such atomization and calculated instrumentality replace relations of enduring diffuse solidarity, so kinship will disappear (whatever the state of biology might be); insofar as rationality is directed toward a restructuring of social ends and the creation of new forms of the societal community, kinship may re-create itself in forms we cannot yet foresee.

BIBLIOGRAPHY

1. U.S. DEPARTMENT OF COMMERCE, *Americans at Mid-Decade*, Series P-23, No. 16 (March, 1966).
2. NELS ANDERSON, *The Hobo* (Chicago: The University of Chicago Press, 1923).
3. FREDERICK BARTH, *Ethnic Groups and Boundaries* (London: George Allen & Unwin, 1969).
4. DANIEL BELL, *Work and Its Discontents: The Cult of Efficiency in America* (Boston: Beacon Press, 1956).
5. NORMAN W. BELL AND EZRA F. VOGEL, *A Modern Introduction to the Family* (Glencoe, Ill.: The Free Press, 1960).
6. J. BEN-DAVID, *The Sociology of Science* (Englewood Cliffs, N.J.: Prentice-Hall, Inc., 1971).
7. BENNETT BERGER, *Working-Class Suburb: A Study of Auto Workers in Suburbia* (Berkeley: University of California Press, 1960).
8. ANDREW BILLINGSLEY, *Black Families in White America* (Englewood Cliffs, N.J.: Prentice-Hall, Inc., 1968).
9. ROBERT BLAUNER, *Alienation and Freedom: The Factory Worker and His Industry* (Chicago: University of Chicago Press, 1964).
10. W. BLOOMBERG AND H. J. SCHMANDT, EDS., *Power, Poverty, and Urban Policy*, Urban Affairs Annual Reviews, Vol. 2 (Beverly Hills, Calif.: Sage Publications Inc., 1968).
11. ELIZABETH BOTT, *Family and Social Network* (London: Tavistock Publications, Ltd., 1956).

12. JAMES BURNHAM, *The Managerial Revolution* (New York: John Day Company, 1941).

13. RICHARD CENTERS, *The Psychology of Social Classes* (Princeton: Princeton University Press, 1949).

14. LOUIS DUMONT, "Caste, Racism and 'Stratification'," *Contributions to Indian Sociology*, No. V (October 1961), pp. 20–43.

15. ———, *Homo Hierarchicus* (Chicago: University of Chicago Press, 1970).

16. EMILE DURKHEIM, *The Division of Labor in Society*, trans. by G. Simpson (Glencoe, Ill.: The Free Press, 1947).

17. FRIEDRICH ENGELS, *The Condition of the Working Class in England* (Stanford, Calif.: Stanford University Press, 1968).

18. MEYER FORTES, *Kinship and the Social Order: The Legacy of Lewis Henry Morgan* (Chicago: Aldine Publishing Co., 1969).

19. ———, "Time and Social Structure: An Ashanti Case Study," in M. Fortes ed., *Social Structure*, Studies Presented to A. R. Radcliffe-Brown (Oxford: Clarendon Press, 1949), pp. 55–84.

20. ———, *The Web of Kinship Among the Tallensi* (New York: Oxford University Press, 1949).

21. JOHN K. GALBRAITH, *The New Industrial State* (Boston: Houghton, Mifflin Co., 1967).

22. HERBERT GANS, *The Levittowners* (New York: Pantheon Books Inc., 1967).

23. ———, *The Urban Villagers* (New York: The Free Press, 1962).

24. H. GARFINKEL, *Studies in Ethnomethodology* (Englewood Cliffs, N.J.: Prentice-Hall, Inc., 1967).

25. P. GASKELL, *Artisans and Machinery* (London: John W. Parker, 1836).

26. TODD GITLIN AND NANCI HOLLANDER, *Uptown: Poor Whites in Chicago* (New York: Harper and Row, Publishers, Inc., 1970).

27. NATHAN GLAZER AND DANIEL P. MOYNIHAN, *Beyond the Melting Pot* (Cambridge, Mass.: M.I.T. Press, 1963).

28. JOHN H. GOLDTHORPE, DAVID LOCKWOOD, FRANK BECHHOFER, AND JENNIFER PLATT, *The Affluent Worker in the Class Structure* (Cambridge: Cambridge University Press, 1969).

29. LEO GREBLER, JOAN W. MOORE AND RALPH C. GUZMAN, *The Mexican-American People* (New York: The Free Press, 1970).
30. JOSEPH GREENBERG, *Language Universals* (The Hague: Mouton & Co., 1966).
31. JÜRGEN HABERMAS, *Toward a Rational Society* (Boston: Beacon Press, 1970).
32. L. HARZ, *The Founding of New Societies* (New York: Harcourt Brace Jovanovich, Inc., 1964).
33. ROBERT W. HODGE AND DONALD J. TREIMAN, "Class Identification in the United States," *American Journal of Sociology*, **73**, 5, 1968.
34. DORIS B. HOLLEB, *Social and Economic Information for Urban Planning* (Chicago: Center for Urban Studies, University of Chicago, 1969).
35. JOHN F. KAIN, "Urban Travel Behaviour," in Leo F. Schnore, and Henry Fagin, eds., *Urban Research and Policy Planning* (Beverly Hills, Calif.: Sage Publications, Inc., 1967).
36. JOHN F. KANTER AND MELVIN ZELNICK, "Sexual Experience of Young Unmarried Women in the United States," *Family Planning Perspectives*, Vol. 4, No. 4, October 1972, pp. 9–18.
37. R. LINCOLN KEISER, *The Vice Lords: Warriors of the Streets* (New York: Holt, Rinehart & Winston, 1969).
38. ARTHUR KORNHAUSER, "Public Opinion and Social Class," *American Journal of Sociology*, **55** (1950), pp. 333–345.
39. JOHN C. LEGGETT, *Class, Race and Labor* (New York: Oxford University Press, 1968).
40. LIONEL S. LEWIS AND DENNIS BRISSETT, "Sex as Work: A Study of Avocational Counseling," *Social Problems*, **15**, No. 1 (1967), pp. 8–17.
41. ELLIOT LIEBOW, *Tally's Corner* (Boston: Little, Brown, 1967).
42. SEYMOUR MARTIN LIPSET, *The First New Nation* (New York: Anchor Books, Doubleday & Company, Inc., 1967).
43. HERBERT MARCUSE, *One-Dimensional Man* (Boston: Beacon Press, 1964).
44. HARRIETT MARTINEAU, *Society in America* (New York: Doubleday & Company, Inc., 1962).

45. KURT MAYER, "The Changing Shape of the American Class Structure," *Social Research*, **30** (1963), pp. 458–468.

46. ELTON MAYO, *The Social Problems of an Industrial Civilization* (Boston: Harvard University Graduate School of Business Administration, 1945).

47. WALTER MILLER, "The Elimination of the Lower Class as National Policy," in Daniel P. Moynihan (ed.), *On Understanding Poverty: Perspectives from the Social Sciences* (New York: Basic Books, Inc., 1969), pp. 260–315.

48. JOHN M. MOGEY, *Family and Neighbourhood* (Oxford: Oxford University Press, 1956).

49. DANIEL P. MOYNIHAN, "Memorandum to President Nixon," printed in *The New York Times*, Sunday, March 1, 1970.

50. GEORGE PETER MURDOCK, *Social Structure* (New York: The Macmillan Company, 1949).

51. GUNNAR MYRDAL, *Challenge to Affluence* (New York: Pantheon Books, Inc., 1963).

52. *The Negro Family: The Case for National Action* (Washington, D.C.: Office of Policy Planning and Research, United States Department of Labor, 1965).

53. TALCOTT PARSONS, *Family, Socialization and Interaction Process* (Glencoe, Ill.: The Free Press, 1955).

54. ———, "The Kinship System of the Contemporary United States" (1943), reprinted in Talcott Parsons, *Essays in Sociological Theory* (Glencoe, Ill.: The Free Press, 1949).

55. ———, *The Social System* (New York: The Free Press, 1951).

56. ———, *Societies* (Englewood Cliffs, N.J.: Prentice-Hall, Inc., 1966).

57. ———, *The System of Modern Societies* (Englewood Cliffs, N.J.: Prentice-Hall, Inc., 1971).

58. ———, E. A. SHILS, K. NAEGLE, AND J. PITTS, eds., *Theories of Society* (New York: The Free Press, 1961).

59. MICHAEL M. POSTAN, *An Economic History of Western Europe, 1945–1964* (London: Methuen, 1967).

60. LEE RAINWATER, *Behind Ghetto Walls* (Chicago: Aldine Publishing Co., 1970).

61. ———, RICHARD P. COLEMAN, AND GERALD HANDEL, *Workingman's Wife* (New York: Oceana Publications, Inc., 1959).

62. DAVID RIESMAN, *The Lonely Crowd* (New Haven: Yale University Press, 1951).

63. HYMAN RODMAN, "The Lower Class Value Stretch," *Social Forces,* **42** (December 1963), pp. 205–215.

64. COLIN ROSSER AND CHRISTOPHER HARRIS, *The Family and Social Change* (London: Routledge & Kegan Paul, 1965).

65. DAVID M. SCHNEIDER, *The History of Public Welfare in New York State, 1867–1940* (Chicago: The University of Chicago Press, 1941).

66. ———, *American Kinship: A Cultural Account* (Englewood Cliffs, N.J.: Prentice-Hall, Inc., 1968).

67. ———, "Kinship Religion and Nationality," in V. Turner (ed.), *Forms of Symbolic Action,* Proceedings of the 1969 Spring Meeting of the American Ethnological Society (Seattle: University of Washington Press, 1969).

68. ———, "What Is Kinship all About?" in P. Reining, *Kinship Studies in the Morgan Centennial Year* (Washington, D.C.: Washington Anthropological Society, 1972), pp. 32–63.

69. JOHN SEELEY, ALEXANDER SIM, AND ELIZABETH W. LOOSLEY, *Crestwood Heights: A Study of the Culture of Suburban Life* (New York: Basic Books, Inc., 1956).

70. EDWARD A. SHILS, "Deference," in John A. Jackson, ed., *Social Stratification* (Cambridge: Cambridge University Press, 1968), pp. 104–132.

71. UPTON SINCLAIR, *The Jungle* (New York: Doubleday & Company, Inc., 1906).

72. RAYMOND T. SMITH, *The Negro Family in British Guiana* (London: Routledge & Kegan Paul, 1956).

73. ———, "The Nuclear Family in Afro-American Kinship," *Journal of Comparative Family Studies,* **1** (Autumn 1970), pp. 55–70.

74. ———, "The Matrifocal Family," in Jack Goody (ed.), *Essays in Kinship* (Cambridge: Cambridge University Press, in Press).

75. M. STACEY, *Tradition and Change: A Study of Banbury* (Oxford: Oxford University Press, 1960).

76. CAROL B. STACK, "The Kindred of Viola Jackson: Residence and Family Organization of an Urban Black American Family," in Whitten and Szwed, eds., *Afro-American Anthropology* (New York: The Free Press, 1970), pp. 303–311.

77. S. THERNSTROM, *Poverty and Progress* (Cambridge, Mass.: Harvard University Press, 1964).

78. WILLIAM I. THOMAS AND FLORIAN ZNANIECKI, *The Polish Peasant in Europe and America* (Boston: Richard G. Badger, The Goreham Press, 1918).

79. ALEXIS DE TOCQUEVILLE, *Democracy in America* (New York: Vintage Books, 1957).

80. EDWARD B. TYLOR, *Anthropology, an Introduction to the Study of Man and Civilization* (New York: D. Appleton & Co., 1916).

81. U.S. BUREAU OF THE CENSUS, *Statistical Abstract of the United States: 1971* (92nd edition), Washington, D.C., 1971.

82. PIERRE DE VISE, *Chicago's Widening Color Gap*, Interuniversity Social Research Committee (Chicago, 1967), Report No. 2.

83. W. LLOYD WARNER, *The Living and the Dead* (New Haven: Yale University Press, 1959).

84. ———, MARCIA MEEKER, AND KENNETH EELLS, *Social Class in America* (New York: Harper Torchbooks, 1960).

85. ———, AND PAUL S. LUNT, *The Social Life of a Modern Community* (New Haven: Yale University Press, 1945).

86. ———, AND PAUL S. LUNT, *The Status System of a Modern Community* (New Haven: Yale University Press, 1941).

87. MAX WEBER, *The Theory of Social and Economic Organization* (Glencoe, Ill.: The Free Press, 1947).

88. WILLIAM H. WHYTE, *The Organization Man* (New York: Simon & Schuster, Inc., 1956).

89. MICHAEL WILLMOTT AND PETER YOUNG, *Family and Kinship in East London* (London: Routledge & Kegan Paul, 1957).

Index